THE RECIPIENT OF CONFIRMATION

A Historical Synopsis and a Commentary

THE CATHOLIC UNIVERSITY OF AMERICA
CANON LAW STUDIES
No. 267

The Recipient of Confirmation

A Historical Synopsis and a Commentary

A DISSERTATION

SUBMITTED TO THE FACULTY OF THE SCHOOL OF CANON LAW OF THE CATHOLIC UNIVERSITY OF AMERICA IN PARTIAL FULFILLMENT OF THE REQUIREMENTS FOR THE DEGREE OF DOCTOR OF CANON LAW

BY THE
REV. J. CLEMENT BENNINGTON, A.B., J.C.L.
PRIEST OF THE ARCHDIOCESE OF PHILADELPHIA

THE CATHOLIC UNIVERSITY OF AMERICA PRESS
WASHINGTON, D. C.
1952

NIHIL OBSTAT:

CLEMENS V. BASTNAGEL

Censor Librorum

deputatus ad hoc

Washington, D. C., die 20a Martii, 1952

IMPRIMATUR:

✠ J. F. O'HARA, C.S.C.

Archiepiscopus Philadelphiensis

Philadelphia, die 21a Martii, 1952

MURRAY & HEISTER
WASHINGTON, D. C.

PRINTED BY
TIMES AND NEWS PUBLISHING CO.
GETTYSBURG, PA., U. S. A.

TABLE OF CONTENTS

TABLE OF CONTENTS (Continued)

FOREWORD

The subject of this dissertation embraces several questions about which much theory has been written. The writer has reviewed this theory, endeavored to derive practical conclusions from it, and to apply these conclusions to particular cases.

The first part of this dissertation contains a historical summary of the questions that are treated in the doctrinal commentary.

In the first chapter of the doctrinal part, the writer considers the question of the necessity of receiving confirmation and how various classes of persons are affected by this necessity. He then treats of the somewhat controverted question of the appropriate age for the reception of confirmation. Succeeding chapters describe the conditions required in the recipient, and the conditions with reference to the time and place for confirmation. The final chapter examines the various problems that can result when confirmation is received from a minister other than a bishop.

The comparatively recent decree of the Sacred Congregation of the Sacraments, *Spiritus Sancti munera,*[1] has been cited wherever the subject matter of the decree coincided with the matter of this thesis.

The writer wishes to express his gratitude on this occasion to His Eminence, Dennis Cardinal Dougherty, the late Archbishop of Philadelphia, for the opportunity of advanced study; to the Faculty of the school of Canon Law; and to all others who in any way have contributed to the completion of this work.

---

[1] *Acta Apostolicae Sedis* (Romae, 1909-1929; Civitate Vaticana, 1929-), XXXVIII (1946), 349.

PART I

Historical Synopsis

CHAPTER I

Institution of the Sacrament of Confirmation

The time when the sacrament of confirmation was instituted is not clearly indicated in the Sacred Scriptures. However, a scrutiny of the whole Gospel story suggests that there are three possibilities as to the occasion which Christ chose to institute this sacrament.[1] The occasion may have been one which took place after his resurrection, and on which he gave to his apostles the fullness of episcopal power, saying to them,

"As the Father has sent me, I also send you. . . . Receive the Holy Spirit."[2]

It is also possible that our Lord instituted confirmation at the Last Supper, at some point of the long discourse which he had with his apostles.[3] Several times during this discourse, Christ promised that he would send the Holy Ghost both to the apostles and to the others of the faithful. It is possible that on this same occasion he taught the manner in which the Holy Ghost was to be conferred upon individuals.[4] On this occasion, however, confirmation could have been instituted only to the extent that Christ would have taught his apostles the matter and form of the sacrament. Since the apostles were not yet bishops, he would not at that time have endowed them with the power to confirm.[5]

---

[1] Cf. Noldin-Schmitt, *Summa Theologiae Moralis iuxta Codicem Iuris Canonici* (26. ed., 3 vols., Ratisbonae: Pustet, 1940), III, n. 84 (henceforth to be referred to with the names of the authors).

[2] John, XX; 21-22; cf. Coronata, *Institutiones Iuris Canonici, De Sacramentis Tractatus Canonicus* (3 vols., Taurini: Marietti, 1943-1946), I, n. 160 (to be referred to hereafter with the name of the author).

[3] John, XIV-XVII.

[4] It was on the basis of this assumption that there was developed the custom of consecrating the chrism of confirmation on Holy Thursday. Cf. Noldin-Schmitt, *loc. cit.*

[5] Cf. Noldin-Schmitt, *loc. cit.*

From this observation a third assumption is possible, viz., that our Lord began the institution of confirmation at the Last Supper, and completed it after his resurrection, when he bestowed upon his apostles the fullness of the priesthood and episcopacy.[6]

Although Sacred Scripture does not point to any definite time as the occasion on which confirmation was instituted, there are to be found in the New Testament two passages which clearly demonstrate that this sacrament was being administered to the faithful during the time of the apostles.[7]

These texts refer to a rite of imposing hands upon the faithful that they might receive the Holy Ghost. This rite, the administration of which was reserved to the apostles, was something distinct from baptism, but presupposed the previous reception of baptism.

Both of these passages are contained in the *Acts of the Apostles.* The first begins at Chapter VIII, 1. The text relates the convert work of Philip the Deacon in Samaria. He had converted many to the faith and baptized them. The text, in verse 14, continues as follows:

"Now when the apostles in Jerusalem heard that Samaria had received the word of God, they sent to them Peter and John. On their arrival they prayed for them, that they might receive the Holy Spirit; for as yet he had not come upon any of them, but they had only been baptized in the name of the Lord Jesus. Then they laid their hands on them and they received the Holy Spirit."

The second of these passages is taken from Chapter XIX, 1-6:

"Now it was while Apollos was in Corinth that Paul, after passing through the upper districts, came to Ephesus and found certain disciples; and he said to them, 'Did you receive the Holy Spirit when you became believers?' But they said to him, 'We have not even heard that there is a Holy Spirit.' And he said, 'How then

---

[6] Cf. Regatillo, *Ius Sacramentarium* (2 vols., Santander: Sal Terrae, 1945-1946), I, n. 78 (henceforth to be referred to with the name of the author).

[7] Cf. O'Dwyer, *Confirmation, A Study in the Development of Sacramental Theology* (New York, 1915), pp. 2-5 (henceforth to be referred to with the name of the author).

were you haptized?' They said, 'With John's baptism.' Then Paul said, 'John baptized the people with a baptism of repentance, telling them to believe in him who was to come after him, that is, in Jesus.' On hearing this they were baptized in the name of the Lord Jesus; and when Paul laid his hands on them, the Holy Spirit came upon them, and they began to speak in tongues and to prophesy."

CHAPTER II

EXISTENCE AND GRAVITY OF THE OBLIGATION TO RECEIVE CONFIRMATION

From the very beginning of the Church confirmation was conferred immediately after the subject had received baptism, and as part of his rite of initiation into membership in the Church. This fact is attested to by Tertullian (ca. 16-ca. 230), one of the earliest of the Christian writers.[1]

Verification of this fact is likewise supplied by letters of two of the early popes. Pope Innocent I (401-417) wrote to Bishop Decentius of Gubbio that the confirmation of infants was manifestly the function of no one other than a bishop.[2] Pope Gregory I (590-604) wrote in the same vein to Januarius, Bishop of Sardinia, in 593. He stated: "Priests are not to presume to sign infants on the forehead with sacred chrism; but priests may administer chrism on the breast, that bishops may afterwards administer it on the forehead."[3]

Although the two letters just mentioned refer to the confirmation of infants, the liturgical books of the early Church show that adults were subject to the same rite of initiation as were infants,

---

[1] *Liber de Baptismo,* cap. VII et VIII, "Egressi de lavacro perungimur benedicta unctione. . . . Dehinc manus imponitur per benedictionem advocans et invitans Spiritum Sanctum."—*Corpus Scriptorum Ecclesiasticorum Latinorum* (71 vols., editum consilio et impensis Academiae Litterarum Caesariae Vindobonae, 1866-), XX, 207 (to be referred to hereafter as *SCEL*).

[2] Jaffé, *Regesta Pontificum Romanorum ab condita Ecclesia ad annum post Christum natum MCXCVIII* (2. ed., G. Wattenbach, F. Kaltenbrunner, P. Ewald, S. Lowenfeld, 2 vols., Lipsiae, 1885-1888), n. 311 (to be referred to hereafter as *Regesta*); Migne, *Patrologiae Cursus Completus, Series Latina* (221 vols., Parisiis, 1844-1864), XX, 555 (to be referred to hereafter as *MPL*).

[3] *Gregorii Registrii Lib. I-IV,* lib. IV, ep. 9—*Monumenta Germaniae Historica Epistolae Epistolarum,* Tom. I, pars I (ed. P. Ewald, Berolini, 1887), 240; Jaffé, *Regesta,* n. 1281.

except that in the case of adults the ceremonies were considerably lengthened.[4]

Among these liturgical books is the Gregorian Sacramentary, which in its ultimate form represents the liturgy in use at the time of Pope Adrian I (772-795).[5] This book describes the administration of confirmation as part of the rite of initiation, which consisted of baptism, confirmation and first Communion.[6] Consequently it appears that if one wished to be formally enrolled as a member of the Church, it was mandatory that he receive the sacrament of confirmation.

Moreover there exist texts, belonging to the early days of the Church, which contemplate the reception of baptism under extraordinary circumstances, apart from the formal rite of initiation. These texts seem to imply a duty to receive confirmation, for they all at least suggest that a man is not yet a perfect Christian until he has been confirmed.

Included among these texts is a letter of Pope Cornelius I (251-253), in which he related that Novatian, after having received baptism on his sick bed, did not also receive the other things which according to the law of the Church he was expected to receive; moreover, he had not been *sealed* by the bishop, and since he had not been a recipient of this sealing, how could he have received the Holy Ghost.[7]

Similarly both the Council of Elvira (ca. 306) and the Council of Arles (314) referred to the need of confirmation in those whose reception of baptism took place on the occasion of illness. The former council included legislation to the effect that while at sea,

---

[4] Cf. Duchesne, *Christian Worship, Its Origin and Evolution* (translated from the Third French Edition by M. L. McClure, New York, 1903), pp. 293-295 (to be referred to hereafter with the name of the author).

[5] Duchesne, p. 125.

[6] Duchesne, p. 314; cf. also *The Gelasian Sacramentary, Liber Sacramentorum Romanae Ecclesiae* (Edited by H. A. Wilson, Oxford, 1894), pp. 86-87; *Ordo Romanus I*—Mabillon, *Museum Italicum* (2. ed., 2 vols., Parisiis, 1724), II, 27.

[7] *Epistola ad Fabium Ep. Antiochenum*, n. 15—Migne, *Patrologiae Cursus Completus, Series Graeca* (161 vols., Parisiis, 1857-1866), XX, 617; Kirch, *Enchiridion Fontium Historiae Ecclesiasticae Antiquae* (4. ed., Friburgi Brisgoviae: Herder, 1923), n. 256.

or at some distance from church, a baptized person who is not a bigamist can himself baptize a person who is suffering from illness, but on the condition that, if the sick person survives, he must be brought to a bishop, who with the imposition of hands will perfect the status of such a person in the faith.[8] Canon 48 of the Council of Arles (314) simply stated that hands should be imposed on those who in sickness had been converted to the faith.[9]

The celebrated controversy regarding the rebaptism of heretics, which took place during the life of St. Cyprian (210-258), is of some value in a study of the recipient of confirmation, inasmuch as it demonstrates that heretics were subject to an obligation to receive confirmation in their process of being reconciled with the Church.

At the time of this controversy two practices were in vogue. At Rome, at Caesarea of Palestine, and also at Alexandria, the baptism conferred by heretics was regarded as valid, so long as the essential rites were performed. The church authorities in reconciling heretics deemed it sufficient, therefore, simply to confer the sacrament of confirmation. In Africa, especially at Carthage, and in the churches of Syria and Asia Minor, the baptism conferred in heresy was deemed invalid, and the whole process of Christian initiation had to be repeated.[10]

St. Cyprian, Bishop of Carthage, argued that there is only one baptism as there is only one Church, one God and one Christ, and this baptism is found only in the unity of the Church. To break with the unity of the Church, then, is to break with baptism, the sacrament of unity.[11] He further contended that his adversaries admitted that confirmation conferred by heretics was invalid, since they repeated that sacrament in the ceremony of reconciliation. Why, he argued, should not a consistent viewpoint be maintained?

---

[8] Canon 38—Mansi, *Sanctorum Consiliorum Nova et Amplissima Collectio* (53 vols. in 60, Parisiis, 1901-1927), II, 12 (to be cited hereafter as Mansi).

[9] Mansi, II, 572.

[10] Cf. Pourrat, *Theology of the Sacraments, a Study in Positive Theology* (Authorized Translation from the third French Edition, 3. ed., London, St. Louis: Herder, 1924), pp. 119 ff. (to be referred to hereafter with the name of the author).

[11] *Epistola LXXIV,* 11—*CSEL,* III, 808-809.

If the rite which confers the Holy Ghost is not considered valid among heretics, then neither should baptism be considered valid.[12]

However, to St. Cyprian's arguments Pope St. Stephen I (254-257) opposed another idea which was based upon the immemorial custom of the Church and which supposed the objective character of the value of baptism. No one, said the Pope, was to rebaptize the heretics that returned to the Church, but there was to be an imposition of hands on them for penance. This was the practice transmitted by the apostles, and this was the practice which was to be observed. For in baptism it was not the worth of the minister that availed. The invocation of the Trinity and of the name of Jesus was sufficient to produce the sanctification of baptism.[13]

The Council of Arles (314), in a canon which ran contrary to the opinion of St. Cyprian, also testified to an obligation on the part of converts from heresy to receive confirmation. The canon stated that these persons were simply to be questioned whether they had been baptized in the name of the Father, of the Son and of the Holy Ghost. In the event of a baptism thus conferred, only the imposition of hands was still necessary.[14]

One of the more explicit references in the early Church to an obligation to receive confirmation is to be found in a canon of the Council of Laodicaea (343-381). This canon stated that those who were illumined through baptism ought afterwards be anointed with heavenly chrism, so as to be partakers of the kingdom of Christ.[15] Substantially the same statement came from the pen of Pope St. Leo the Great (440-461) in the following century.[16] In a letter written in 458 to Nicetas, Bishop of Aquileia, he indicated

[12] *Epistola LXXIV*, 5—*CSEL*, III, 802-803.

[13] Cf. Denzinger-Bannwart-Umberg, *Enchiridion Symbolorum Definitionum et Declarationum* (ed. 21-23, Friburgi Brisgoviae: Herder, 1937), nn. 46-47, and appended footnotes (to be cited hereafter as *Enchiridion*); Pourrat, *loc. cit.*

[14] Canon 8—Mansi, II, 472.

[15] Canon 48—Mansi, II, 572.

[16] Cap. LX, n. 48, *Appendix ad S. Leonis Magni Opera seu Codex Canonum Ecclesiasticorum et Constitutionum Sanctae Sedis Apostolicae Omnium qui huc usque prodierunt Vetustissimus*—*MPL*, LVI, 719-720.

that in such cases only the invocation of the Holy Spirit through the imposition of hands was necessary.[17]

Three texts which imply an obligation to receive confirmation are particularly noteworthy because of the unusual circumstances connected with them.

The first of these texts is a canon attributed by Burchard (+ 1025) and other compilers to a Council of Orleans, to the effect that those who are old enough should come fasting to receive confirmation, and should be admonished to confess their sins beforehand, in order that cleansed from their sins they might be worthy to receive the Holy Ghost, since one is not completely a Christian until one has been anointed by means of episcopal confirmation.[18] However, while this canon is not to be found among the early councils of Orleans,[19] it does appear among the *Diocesan Capitula* compiled in 858 by Herardus, Archbishop of Tours (855-870).[20] It seems that this decree was incorrectly labeled by Burchard, and that subsequent compilers perpetuated the error by relying on his authority.[21]

The second of these texts is a letter, pseudo-Isidorian in origin, and attributed to Pope Urban I (222-230), which found its way into the works of the medieval compilers, and eventually also into the *Decree of Gratian.*[22] This letter stated that upon the reception of baptism all the faithful should receive the Holy Ghost through the imposition of the hands of the bishop, in order that they might be found to be Christians in the full sense of the word.

The third text was another letter, this time attributed to Pope Melchiades (311-314), and supposedly written to certain bishops

---

[17] Jaffé, *Regesta,* n. 536; Mansi, VI, 331.

[18] Burchard, *Decretum,* lib. IV, canon 60—*MPL,* CXL, 738; Ivo, *Panormia,* lib. I, cap. 119—*MPL,* CLXI, 1071.

[19] Cf. Bruns, *Canones Apostolorum et Conciliorum IV, V, VI, VII* (2 vols., Berlin, 1839), II, 160-208.

[20] *Capitula Herardi,* canon 75—*MPL,* CXXI, 769.

[21] Cf. Van Hove, *Commentarium Lovaniense,* Vol. I, Tom. I, *Prolegomena ad Codicem Iuris Canonici* (2. ed., Mechliniae-Romae: H. Dessain, 1945), p. 320 (to be referred to hereafter as *Prolegomena*).

[22] C. 1, D.V, de cons.; Jaffé, *Regesta,* n. 87; Ivo, *Panormia,* lib. I, cap. 123—*MPL,* CLXI, 1041.

in Spain.[23] In this letter Pope Melchiades is represented as answering the question which of the two sacraments, baptism or confirmation, was the greater. He accordingly stated in his letter that both are great sacraments, but that since confirmation can be administered only by the higher prelates and not by those of lesser rank, it ought to be held in greater veneration. He added that these two sacraments are so linked together that, unless death comes between them, one cannot rightly be administered without the other.

Although this letter and the letter attributed to Pope Urban are now known not to have been authentic, yet because of their acceptance as papal letters, in view of their attribution to these early popes, they were frequently quoted, or at least referred to, by the later councils.[24]

After the time of the appearance of the *Decree of Gratian* (ca. 1140) testimony regarding the obligation to receive confirmation began to be more explicit.

Prior to that time the learned Hugh of St. Victor (1096-1141) had included in his writings the opinion that it would be altogether dangerous to depart from this life without having received confirmation.[25]

St. Thomas Aquinas (ca. 1225-1274) commented upon this opinion. He agreed with Hugh of St. Victor that it would be dangerous to leave this life without having been confirmed, not because one would be damned for that reason, unless there was contempt for the sacrament, but because the soul would be deprived of a perfection it would otherwise possess. Thus, sinless children who died upon having received confirmation attained to a greater degree of glory than if they died without the sacrament.[26]

Beginning with the early part of the thirteenth century, there were a number of councils the decrees of which imposed a duty

---

[23] C. 3, D.V, de cons.; Jaffé, *Regesta,* n. 171; Anselm of Lucca, *Collectio Canonum una cum Collectione Minore* (ed. F. Thaner, Oeniponte, 1906-1915), lib. IX, c. 23; Burchard, *Decretum,* lib. IV, canon 66—*MPL,* CXL, 738.

[24] Cf. Van Hove, *Prolegomena,* pp. 309-311.

[25] *De Sacramentis,* lib. II, pars VII, canon 3—*MPL,* CLXXVI, 462.

[26] *Summa Theologica,* Pars III, q. 72, a. 8, ad 4.

upon parents to have their children confirmed, and obedience to these decrees was enforced by means of penal sanctions. However, these laws were purely local in character. They did not bind except within the confines of the respective territories for which they were enacted.

Richardus Anglicus (Richard Poore, + 1237), Bishop of Salisbury (1217-1228), ordered his priests to warn the people frequently regarding the need of having their children confirmed. He further stated that should parents through neglect or carelessness not have their children receive confirmation within five years after birth, then both the mother and the father were to be denied admission to the church until they had fulfilled their duty. He likewise subjected to penalties any and all of his priests who were negligent in the matter of duly providing for the reception of this sacrament by the children of the parishes over which they ruled.[27]

The Council of Worcester (1240) went a step further in an effort to prevent parental neglect with respect to the sacrament of confirmation. It charged pastors to inform the fathers and mothers that, when the opportunity was present and they did not have their children confirmed within a year after their birth, they were to be denied admission to church.[28]

One of the more rigorous punishments for parents who neglected to provide for the confirmation of their children was legislated by the Council of Exeter in 1287. It decreed that, with opportunity permitting, parents were to have their children receive the sacrament within three years after birth. If the parents proved remiss in this matter, they were to be required to fast on bread and water every Friday until their obligation was discharged.[29]

As to adults who were guilty of neglect as regards their own reception of confirmation, the IV Council of Milan (1576), presided over by St. Charles Borromeo (1538-1584), decreed that such offenders should be subject to canonical discipline,[30] whereas the Council of Bourges (1584) urged that the faithful be fore-

---

[27] *Constitutions of Richard Poore, Bishop of Salisbury,* canon XXIV—Mansi, XXII, 1114.

[28] Canon 6—Mansi, XXIII, 527.

[29] Canon 3—Mansi, XXIV, 787.

[30] Pars II, cap. 3—Mansi, XXXIV A, 221.

warned that no one was to be admitted to the sacraments of the Eucharist and of matrimony when the lack of being confirmed had resulted through personal neglect.[31]

Other councils, without invoking any threat of penal sanction, urged a more widespread administration of confirmation.[32] These councils stressed the importance of the pastors' instructing of the faithful as to the nature, dignity and efficacy of the sacrament, and the consequent respect that was due to it.[33] Pastors and preachers of the word of God were exhorted to warn the people that the sacrament of confirmation could not be neglected or deferred by those who wished to be accounted as true Christians.[34]

The XVII Ecumenical Council, the concluding sessions of which were held at Florence (1438-1445), forcibly insisted on the importance of confirmation. It pointed to the effect of this sacrament as the imparting of the Holy Spirit unto strength, even as He was imparted to the apostles on the day of Pentecost, in order that the Christian might bravely confess the name of Christ. Accordingly, the one to be confirmed was to be anointed on the forehead, where the sense of shame is harbored, in order that he might not flinch from the profession of the name of Christ and especially of his cross, which according to the Apostle (I Cor., 1:23) was to the Jews a source of discouragement and to the Gentiles nought but mere folly. On this account it was that the recipient became marked with the sign of the cross.[35]

The Council of Trent (1545-1563) treated of the sacrament of confirmation in its seventh session. While the Council did not speak of the duty to receive confirmation, it did emphasize the sacramental character of confirmation and anathematized those

---

[31] Canon 8—Mansi, XXXIV A, 889.

[32] Cf. V Council of Milan (1579), Pars I, cap. 8—Mansi, XXXIV A, 363; Council of Rheims (1583), cap. 9—Mansi, XXXIV A, 690; Council of Bordeaux (1583), cap. 10—Mansi, XXXIV A, 756.

[33] Cf. Council of Arles (1260), canon 3—Mansi, XXIII, 1004; Council of Rheims (1583), cap. 9—Mansi, XXXIV A, 690; Council of Benevento (1639), Tit. XXXVI, canon 10—Mansi, XXXVI ter, 585.

[34] Council of Rheims (1583), cap. 9—*loc. cit.;* Council of Bordeaux (1583), cap. 10—Mansi, XXXIV A, 756.

[35] Denzinger, *Enchiridion,* n. 697.

who taught that confirmation after baptism was an idle and empty ceremony, or that of old it was nothing more than an instruction, whereby those who were approaching adolescence gave an account of their faith to the Church.[36]

However, the catechism which was issued by command of the Council was much more complete in detail.[37] This work stated that if ever the diligence of pastors was required in explaining the sacrament of confirmation, that time was the present, "when this sacrament is altogether omitted by many in the holy Church of God, whilst there are very few who study to derive therefrom the fruit of grace which they ought."[38]

As to the necessity of confirmation and the existence of an obligation to receive it, it was explained that this sacrament was not so necessary that one cannot be saved without it; yet it ought not to be omitted by anyone, and the greatest care should be taken in the avoidance of all neglect; for what God has proposed in common to all for their sanctification, all should likewise most earnestly desire.[39]

After the Council of Trent, the question of the obligation to receive confirmation became a subject of considerable speculation. While it was generally agreed that such an obligation did exist, there was difference of opinion as to whether this obligation was of a serious nature.[40]

The divergent views on this question are described in the writings of St. Alphonsus (1696-1787), the outstanding moral theologian of the eighteenth century.[41]

---

[36] Sess. VII, *De sacramento confirmationis,* canon 1—Denzinger, *Enchiridion,* n. 871.

[37] Cf. *Catechism of the Council of Trent* (translated by the Very Rev. J. Donovan, Dublin: James Duffy and Co., Ltd., 1906), Part II, Chapter III, pp. 175-186.

[38] *Ibid.,* p. 175.

[39] *Ibid.,* p. 182.

[40] Cf. Dens, *Tractatus de Sacramentis in Genere et de Sacramentis Baptismi et Confirmationis in Specie* (Mechliniae, 1860), pp. 238-240 (henceforth to be referred to with the name of the author).

[41] *Theologia Moralis* (4 vols., ed. L. Gaudé, Romae: Typis Polyglottis Vaticanis, 1905-1912), lib. VI, n. 60 (hereafter to be referred to with the name of the author).

According to the more lenient opinion there existed means other than confirmation, such as the frequent reception of Holy Communion, the earnest use of prayer and the practice of penance that could secure the strength of soul which otherwise normally resulted from the reception of confirmation, and that moreover there was no strict precept compelling one to receive it. Hence, according to this view, the willful non-reception of this sacrament was regarded as sinful in only three instances, namely, when the foregoing of its reception was due to contempt, when scandal would thereby be given, so as to involve a similar contempt in others, and when charity to oneself demanded that one receive, as, for example, when one was persuaded that he would otherwise lose his faith.

According to the more strict opinion, a serious obligation was present whenever a ready opportunity was offered for its reception, the reason being that all Christians were required to attain the fullness of perfection of the Christian life, and that otherwise they would suffer serious spiritual detriment, especially in times of temptation, if they did not avail themselves of the reception of this sacrament.[42]

During the same century in which St. Alphonsus was writing, impetus was given to the speculation by the appearance of two documents of the Holy See, which appeared to provide added weight for the more strict opinion.

The first of these was the Constitution *Etsi pastoralis* of Pope Benedict XIV (1740-1758), in which he legislated regarding those who had been confirmed by Greek priests of the Italo-Albanian rite who did not possess the required faculties for conferring confirmation.[43] The Pope declared that in such cases the parties were not to be put under constraint to receive confirmation from the bishop if in consequence of such constraint scandals could arise, since the sacrament of confirmation was not of such a necessity that one could not be saved without it. However, the people were

---

[42] Cf. St. Alphonsus, *loc. cit.*

[43] 26 maii 1742, § III, n. IV—*Codicis Iuris Canonici Fontes* (cura Emi Petri Card. Gasparri editi, 9 vols., Romae [postea Civitate Vaticana]: Typis Polyglottis Vaticanis, 1923-1939. Vols. VII, VIII, IX ed. cura et studio Emi Iustiani Card. Serédi), n. 328 (to be referred to hereafter as *Fontes*).

to be taught by their ordinaries that they were held guilty of grave sin if, while they were able to approach the sacrament of confirmation, they yet refused or neglected to do so.

The second document was an Instruction of the Sacred Congregation for the Propagation of the Faith to the priests who by indult possessed the power to confer confirmation.[44] It was stated in this Instruction that, although this sacrament is not necessary as an indispensably necessary means for salvation, yet it cannot be refused or neglected without the guilt of grave sin in the face of an available opportunity for receiving it.

Although these two documents are cited by some modern authors in support of the existence of a grave obligation to receive confirmation,[45] they are more commonly rejected as factors substantiating this claim.[46]

The Council of New Granada, Colombia (1868), provided that those who had not been confirmed were subject to certain disabilities. The Council enacted that the unconfirmed were not to be permitted to perform the function of sponsor, to wear the religious habit, to receive tonsure or any ecclesiastical orders.[47]

---

[44] 4 maii 1774—*Fontes,* n. 4565.

[45] Cf. Aertnys-Damen, *Theologia Moralis Secundum S. Alfonsum de Ligorio* (14. ed., 2 vols., Taurini: Marietti, 1944), II, n. 92 (to be referred to hereafter with the names of the authors); Marc-Gestermann-Raus, *Institutiones Morales Alphonsionae* (18. ed., 2 vols., Lugdini: Vitte, 1927), II, n. 1501 (hereafter referred to with the names of the authors).

[46] Cf. Coronato, I, n. 173; Noldin-Schmitt, I, n. 93.

[47] Tit. IV, cap. 3—*Acta et Decreta Sacrorum Conciliorum Recentiorum, Collectio Lacensis* (7 vols., Friburgi Brisgoviae (1870-1890), VI, 502 (to be referred to hereafter as *Coll. Lac.*).

CHAPTER III

The Age for the Reception of Confirmation

In the first centuries of the Church the normal practice was to administer confirmation to both adult converts and to infants immediately after their baptism. That this was the ordinarily prevailing custom is revealed in the liturgical books of the early Church, which describe the rite of initiation for both infants and adults as consisting of the reception of baptism, confirmation and Holy Communion.[1]

At first, apparently, this practice was deviated from only when baptism was conferred under exceptional circumstances, for example, when baptism was received in time of illness,[2] or as a member of a heretical sect.[3]

The custom of bestowing baptism and confirmation on the same occasion is retained today in the Oriental Church, and is even permitted in some few places in the Western Church, on the basis of immemorial custom.[4]

However, it appears that as early as the fourth or fifth cen-

---

[1] Cf. *The Gelasian Sacramentary, Liber Sacramentorum Romanae Ecclesiae,* pp. 86-87; *Ordo Romanus I*—Mabillon, *Museum Italicum,* II, 27; Duchesne, pp. 125, 292-295, 314; Villien, *The History and Liturgy of the Sacraments* (English Translation by H. W. Edwards, London: Burns, Oates and Washburn, Ltd., 1932), pp. 1-47 (henceforth to be cited with the name of the author); Mourret, *A History of the Catholic Church* (translated by Newton Thompson, 6 vols., St. Louis and London: Herder, 1930-1946), I, 281-285 (henceforth to be cited as Mourret-Thompson).

[2] Cf. Cornelius I (251-253), *Epistola ad Fabium ep. Antiochenum,* n. 15—Kirch, *Enchiridion Fontium Historicae Ecclesiasticae Antiquae,* n. 256; Council of Elvira (ca. 306), canon 38—Mansi, II, 12; Council of Arles (314), canon 6—Mansi, II, 471.

[3] Council of Arles (314), canon 8—Mansi, II, 472; Leo I (440-461), *Epistola ad Nicetam*—Jaffé, *Regesta,* n. 536; Villien, p. 67.

[4] Cf. Coronata, I, 174.

tury rural churches in the West had already begun to deviate from this traditional practice.[5]

St. Jerome (342-420) is a witness to this assertion in a statement asknowledging that it was the custom of the churches that the bishop visit the distant communities, and there impose hands on those who had been baptized by priests or deacons.[6]

Further testimony to this effect is furnished by the letter of Pope Innocent I (401-417) to Bishop Decentius of the diocese of Gubbio.[7] This pope stated that with regard to the confirmation of infants it was manifest that it should not be done by anyone but a bishop. The pope then went on to state that priests baptizing *either in the absence or presence of the bishop* are allowed to anoint with chrism those whom they baptize provided it be consecrated by the bishop; but they are not to mark the forehead with the same oil, since this is the privilege only of bishops when they communicate the Holy Ghost.

From this statement it is clear that in this instance the conferral of baptism apart from a time when the bishop could be present to confirm, and apparently under ordinary circumstances, is both recognized and authorized. It is to be noted, also, that the reference is to a confirmation of infants.

A testimony similar to that of Pope Innocent was provided by Pope Gregory I (590-604) in a letter written in 593 to Januarius, Bishop of Sardinia.[8] Pope Gregory wrote that priests were not to presume to sign infants on the forehead with sacred chrism; but they could administer the unction on the breast, so that bishops might afterwards administer the unction on the forehead.

From the letter of Pope Innocent I previously cited it appears evident that the administration of chrism on the breast referred

---

[5] Cf. Reichel, *Complete Manual of Canon Law,* Vol. I, *The Sacraments* (London: John Hodges, 1896), p. 51 (henceforth to be cited with the name of the author); Mourret-Thompson, III, 221.

[6] *Dialogus adversus Luciferanos:* "Non quidem abnuo hanc esse Ecclesiarum consuetudinem ut ad eos qui longe a maioribus urbibus per presbyteros et diacanos baptizati sunt, episcopus ad invocationem Sancti Spiritus manum impositurus excurrat."—*MPL,* XXIII, 164; cf. Reichel, *loc. cit.*

[7] Jaffé, *Regesta,* n. 311; *MPL,* XX, 555.

[8] *Epistola (IX) ad Januarium*—Jaffé, *Regesta,* n. 1281.

to the ceremony of baptism, while the signing on the forehead was a reference to the administration of confirmation.

It is probable that the separation of the two sacraments gradually became more widespread, as the simple priest became the ordinary minister of baptism.[9]

A canon was included among the *Diocesan Capitula* compiled in 858 by Herardus, Archbishop of Tours, which suggests that in this diocese confirmation was more commonly received only by adults. This canon stated that those who were old enough should come fasting to receive confirmation, and should be admonished to confess their sins beforehand, in order that cleansed from their sins they might be worthy to receive the gift of the Holy Ghost, since one is not fully a Christian until he has been anointed by means of episcopal confirmation.[10]

It is not reasonable to assume that this recommendation referred solely to adult converts, since that was not expressly stated in the canon. Moreover, this text appeared among the works of the medieval compilers and consequently it probably influenced the practice in other localities.[11]

Similarly, an excerpt from a sermon of St. Otto of Bamberg (1106-1139) indicates that the practice in his territory was a radical departure from the custom of providing children with confirmation during their period of infancy. In this sermon St. Otto declared that confirmation was necessary for fortifying the faithful with the spiritual vigor of the Holy Ghost, and he recommended that this sacrament should not be deferred until a person had advanced in years, but that it should be received during the period of adolescence, since at that age man was subject to strong temptations.[12]

Nevertheless it is evident that the custom of confirming infants prevailed at least in some places during the thirteenth century, for during that time there were enacted in these localities

---

[9] Cf. Villien, p. 67.

[10] *Capitula Herardi,* canon 75—*MPL,* CXXI, 769.

[11] Cf. Burchard, *Decretum,* lib. IV, canon 60—*MPL,* CXL, 738; Ivo, *Panormia,* lib. I, cap. 119—*MPL,* CLXI, 1071.

[12] *Sermo—MPL,* CLXXIII, 1358.

laws which allowed periods of from one to five years after the birth of children within which parents were required to have their offspring confirmed, or else render themselves liable to the infliction of ecclesiastical penalties.[13]

A reference to the confirmation of infants was made in 1260 by the Council of Arles. This council had ruled that reverence for the sacrament required that ordinarily both the minister and the recipient be fasting when confirmation was conferred, but an exception to this rule obtained in the case of the bishop if the number of recipients was so large that he could not observe the fast, and in the case of infants who needed to be suckled at the mother's breast.[14]

The Council of Cologne in 1280 was the first to mention the age of seven years as the age at which children were to be admitted to confirmation.[15] Apparently from that time onward the custom of deferring the administration of the sacrament until the age of reason became increasingly more common, for in 1457 the Council of Avignon indicated that the tendency away from the custom of confirming infants had become so pronounced that many doubted the licitness of this practice. Because of these doubts the Council decided that confirmation could be administered to infants only if the proper bishop gave his consent to this procedure.[16]

The Council of Cologne in 1536 hesitated to condemn the practice of confirming infants, but pointed out that a more fruitful reception could be had if the recipient were sufficiently advanced in years to confess his sins, to mortify himself by fasting, and to profit by instruction.[17]

However, during the sixteenth and seventeenth centuries the practice of deferring the conferral of confirmation until the age

---

[13] Cf. *Constitutions of Richard Poore, Bishop of Salisbury*, canon XXIV—Mansi, XXII, 1114; Council of Worcester (1240), canon 6—Mansi, XXIII, 527; Council of Exeter (1287), canon 3—Mansi, XXIV, 787.

[14] Canon 3—Mansi, XXIII, 1004.

[15] Canon 5—Mansi, XXIV, 349.

[16] Canon 15—Mansi, XXXII, 187.

[17] Pars septima, canon 9—Mansi, XXXII, 1258.

of discretion prevailed almost universally. This was evident from the many laws which explicitly forbade the confirming of infants.[18]

Further evidence that the policy of confirming infants had for the most part been abandoned was had both in the decrees which required that the reception of confirmation be preceded by confession, or at least accompanied with sorrow for one's sins.[19] and in the laws which specified the degree of religious knowledge that was expected to be present in prospective recipients.[20]

The Catechism of the Council of Trent, in treating of the age for the reception of confirmation, gave a reason of fittingness for delaying the conferral of the sacrament until the time of discretion had been reached. The Catechism stated that until children had reached the use of reason the administration of confirmation was inexpedient. "Wherefore if not to be postponed until the age of twelve, it is most proper to defer it at least to the age of seven; for confirmation has not been instituted as necessary to salvation, but that by virtue thereof we may be found very well armed and prepared, when called upon to fight for the faith of Christ; and for this kind of conflict assuredly no one will consider children, who still want the use of reason, to be qualified."[21]

---

[18] Council of Capua (1569), *De Confirmatione*—Mansi, XXXV A, 710; Council of Milan (1579), pars II, cap. 8—Mansi, XXXIV A, 363; Council of Bourges (1584), canon 6—Mansi, XXXIV A, 889; Council of Aix (1585), *De Conf. Sacr.*—Mansi, XXXIV B, 946; Council of Benevento (1639), tit. XXXVI, canon 15—Mansi, XXXVI ter, 586.

[19] Council of Cologne (1536), pars septima, canon 9—Mansi, XXXII, 1258; Council of Besançon (1571), canon 3—Mansi, XXXVI bis, 52; IV Council of Milan (1576), pars II, cap. 3—Mansi, XXXIV A, 221; Council of Rouen (1581), *De Sacr. Conf.*—Mansi, XXXIV A, 623-624; Council of Rheims (1583), cap. 9—Mansi, XXXIV A, 690; Council of Bordeaux (1583), cap. 10—Mansi, XXXIV A, 756; Council of Bourges (1584), canon 6—Mansi, XXXIV A, 889; Council of Aix (1585), *De Conf. Sacr.*—Mansi, XXXIV B, 946-947.

[20] V Council of Milan (1579), pars I, cap. 8—Mansi, XXXIV A, 363: Council of Rouen (1581), *De Sacr. Conf.*—Mansi, XXXIV A, 623-624; Council of Rheims (1583), cap. 13—Mansi, XXXIV A, 690; Council of Bourges (1584), canon 6—Mansi, XXXIV A, 889; Council of Aix (1585), *De Conf. Sacr.*—Mansi, XXXIV B, 946-947; Council of Benevento (1639), tit. XXXVI, canon 15—Mansi, XXXVI ter, 585-586.

[21] P. 183.

The eighteenth century was an important one in so far as legislation on the age for the reception of confirmation was concerned. Official pronouncements of the Holy See stated at what age the sacrament should normally be received, but at the same time conceded that under certain conditions the administration of confirmation to infants would be justified.

In one of his Instructions, Pope Benedict XIV (1740-1758) observed that the custom, as current in the Oriental Church, of simultaneously conferring baptism and confirmation still prevailed in some dioceses of the Latin Church. This custom, he declared, was altogether to be abrogated, and confirmation was to be conferred only at such an age when the subject duly understood that baptism and confirmation differ one from the other, even as in natural life generation differs from growth.[22]

The import of this Instruction was further determined in an encyclical to the Prefect of the Apostolic Mission in Egypt and to the missionaries associated with him in this Coptic Mission. It was stated that the sacrament of confirmation was not to be conferred on those who had not yet reached the age of seven, unless there was imminent a danger of death in consequence of which the subject, by succumbing to the sickness, would depart from this life without the benefit of the sacrament.[23]

In the year 1774 further enlightenment on this point was provided by a reply of the Sacred Congregation of the Council to a letter from the Bishop of Segovia in Spain.[24] The bishop proposed the question whether confirmation might be administered, not only to adults who enjoyed the use of reason, but also to children who had not yet reached the age of reason. He explained that in Spain the adults could scarcely be brought together during the episcopal visitation, and be prepared by means of a sacramental confession

---

[22] Instr. *Eo quamvis tempore,* 4 maii 1745, § 6. ". . . conferretur sacramentum confirmationis in ea solum aetate, in qua fideles, evacuatis quae erant parvuli, intelligerent, tantum inter se differre baptismum et confirmationem, quantum in naturali vita distat generatio ab incremento."—*Fontes,* n. 357.

[23] Ep. encycl. *Anno vertente,* 19 iun. 1750, § 4—*Fontes,* n. 407.

[24] 12 mart., 23 apr., 1774—*Fontes,* n. 3788.

for the reception of the sacrament of confirmation, unless the visitation be drawn out over many days, inasmuch as the people lived in very scattered communities in the mountains and valleys throughout the diocese. He thought it desirable that the bishops of Spain confer the sacrament to children as well as to adults.

He stated that the custom of administering confirmation immediately after baptism prevailed up to the thirteenth century, and that therefore the age of the recipient did not seem to stand in the way of special consideration that might be given to children of tender years or even to infants. In support of this statement he referred to ancient writers, to ritual books and to the statutes of certain diocesan synods.

He stated that the current law, namely, of not confirming those who were not yet capable of receiving instruction, was not such that it could not yield to grave and urgent causes in warrant of a divergent practice. He thought that, in addition to the danger of death, other causes would qualify as grave and urgent. Among these were the foreseen absence of the bishop for a long time, the advanced age of the bishop, the difficulty of travel, and the great distance from the episcopal city. All these considerations made it difficult to contact again those who had not received confirmation at an earlier episcopal visit. The bishop accordingly asked:

1. In the light of the peculiar circumstances mentioned, may the sacrament of confirmation be administered to children and infants even when they have not attained the use of reason?

2. May the sacrament be administered to such children and infants when they are in danger of death?

While the answer was given in the affirmative to the first question, its affirmative character was conditioned on the presence of the contemplated grave and urgent circumstances, regarding the existence of which all responsible judgment rested on the bishop's conscience. The answer to the second question was given in an unqualified and absolute affirmative.

Shortly after this response was given, a general rule to be observed regarding the age for receiving confirmation was stated succinctly by the Sacred Congregation for the Propagation of the Faith in an Instruction sent to priests who enjoyed the faculty to bestow confirmation.[25] The Sacred Congregation stated that it was fitting for confirmation to be deferred until the recipient is seven years of age, unless the danger of death or some other just cause warrants an exception to this rule.

At the turn of the century the Synod of the Vicariate of Suchow (1803) called attention to what it considered a reasonable cause for a departure from the Church's discipline in ordinary circumstances as regards the age for the reception of confirmation.[26] The Synod declared it licit to confirm children before the age of seven, in view of the peculiar conditions of that territory, which was frequently subject to persecutions and other vicissitudes, and in view of the danger that otherwise the people would be deprived for prolonged periods of so great a benefit as confirmation.

A question of some magnitude was brought to light in the middle of the nineteenth century when a number of provincial councils ruled for their territories that children were not to be confirmed until they had made their first Communion.

The Council of Avignon (1849) stated that it was the rule in the Latin Church for children not to receive confirmation before the age of seven. In the province of Avignon, in addition, they were not to receive confirmation until after their first Communion, except in certain cases wherein the bishop had decided otherwise.[27]

The Council of Tours (1849) declared that with a view to deriving for the faithful a greater benefit from confirmation no one should be admitted to its reception if he had not made his first Communion, unless a grave reason should, in the judgment of the bishop, determine differently.[28]

The Council of Sens (1850) felt persuaded that after their first Holy Communion children could gain a more advanced degree of understanding regarding the sacrament of confirmation, and in

---

[25] Instr. 4 maii 1774—*Fontes,* n. 4565; cf. also, S.C.S. Off. (Vic. Ap. Sandwic.) 11 dec. 1850, ad 12—*Fontes,* n. 913.

[26] Sess. I, cap. 3—*Coll. Lac.,* VI, 599.

[27] Tit. IV, cap. 3—*Coll. Lac.,* IV, 337.

[28] Decretum XVII, n. 2: "Ut uberiores ex suscepta confirmatione fructus percipiant fideles sancimus nullum ad hoc sacramentum admittendum esse, quin ad primam communionem accesserit; nisi tamen aliud gravis ratio judicio Episcopi suadeat."—*Coll. Lac.,* IV, 275.

consequence foster a deeper sense of piety for it, and accordingly were to be made to await this period in their life for the more fruitful reception of the sacrament.[29] However, in a response to the bishop of St. Dennis, dated March 10, 1854, the Sacred Congregation of the Council specified the correct order of temporal succession to be observed in the reception of confirmation and first Communion. The Council stated that previously confirmation should be given, and later on, in due time, first Holy Communion should be provided.[30]

Moreover, at a later time Pope Leo XIII (1878-1903) decided in a way that ran counter to the reasoning of these councils. He declared that it was through confirmation that man was advanced spiritually to maturity and that, having received this sacrament, youths would thereby be more apt to draw richer rewards from the reception of the Eucharist. He stated that the somewhat firmly entrenched custom of conferring confirmation only on condition of the recipient's previous reception of first Holy Communion was to be abrogated.[31]

---

[29] Tit. III, cap. 3—*Coll. Lac.*, IV, 889; cf. also Council of Auch (1850), Tit. III, cap. 1, n. 2—*Coll. Lac.*, IV, 1185; Council of Rouen (1850), Decr. XIV—*Coll. Lac.*, IV, 528; Council of Toulouse (1850), Tit. III, cap. 1—*Coll. Lac.*, IV, 1053; Council of Vienna (1858), Tit. III, cap. 3—*Coll. Lac.*, V, 162; Council of Prague (1860), Tit. IV, cap. 3—*Coll. Lac.*, V, 493.

[30] ". . . prius locus sit confirmationi, postea vero, opportuno tempore, primae Communioni suppeditandae."—*Collectanea S. Congregationis de Propaganda Fide* (2 vols., Romae: Typographia Polyglotta S. C. de Propaganda Fide, 1907), I, n. 1105.

[31] Ep. *Abrogata,* 22 iun. 1897—*Fontes,* n. 634.

CHAPTER IV

Conditions Required in the Recipient of Confirmation

ARTICLE 1. FOR THE VALID RECEPTION OF THE SACRAMENT

The texts of the Sacred Scripture which speak of the administration of confirmation explicitly state that the recipients of this sacrament had been previously baptized.[1] In addition, the liturgical books of the early Church bear witness to the fact that in the rite of initiation confirmation was always preceded by the reception of baptism and was regarded as the complement of this sacrament.[2] Moreover, in many cases when the Fathers and Councils of the early Church spoke of the administration of confirmation they either explicitly or implicitly referred to the reception of baptism which had previously taken place.[3]

From the texts of Scripture, from the practice of the Church, and from the statements of the Fathers and Councils, it appears that the reception of baptism was understood to be a fundamental requisite for the reception of the other sacraments, as was later defined by the Council of Florence (1438-1445).[4]

---

[1] Acts, VIII; 1-17: XIX; 1-6; cf. O'Dwyer, pp. 2-5.

[2] Cf. *The Gelasian Sacramentary, Liber Sacramentorum Romanae Ecclesiae,* pp. 86-87; *Ordo Romanus I*—Mabillon, *Museum Italicum,* II, 27; Villien, pp. 46-47; Duchesne, pp. 292-295; Galtier, "L'Age de la Confirmation," *Nouvelle Revue Théologique* (*NRT*) (Paris, 1869-), LX (1933), 675-686.

[3] Cf. Cornelius I (251-253), *Epistola ad Fabium, ep. Antiochenum,* n. 15—Kirch, *Enchiridion Fontium Historicae Ecclesiae Antiquae,* n. 256; Gregory I (590-604), *Epistola* (*IX*) *ad Januarium*—Jaffé, *Regesta,* n. 1281; Leo I (440-461), *Epistola ad Nicetam*—Jaffé, *Regesta,* n. 536; Council of Elvira (ca. 306), canon 38—Mansi, II, 12; Council of Arles (314), canon 6—Mansi, II, 471; Council of Laodicaea (343-381), canon 48—Mansi, II, 572.

[4] *Decretum pro Armenis* (de sacramentis): "Primum omnium sacramentorum locum tenet sanctum baptisma, quod vitae spiritualis ianua est: per ipsum enim membra Christi ac de corpore efficimus Ecclesiae. . . ."—Denzinger, *Enchiridion,* n. 696; cf. Doronzo, *De Sacramentis in Genere* (Milwaukee: Bruce, 1946), p. 365.

In the celebrated controversy regarding the rebaptism of heretics,[5] it is to be noted that the question at issue was the validity of the baptism received in heresy, and that the converts from heresy were admitted to the rites of confirmation only because it was concluded that the baptism they had received was valid.[6]

This controversy brought out the fact that, while the reception of baptism is a prerequisite for the valid reception of confirmation, to fulfill this demand baptism need not necessarily be received by a person as a member of the Church, for the conferral of baptism by a member of any sect is valid, so long as the proper matter and form are observed and the right intention is had.[7]

For a development of this point the Church is greatly indebted to the doctrine of St. Augustine (354-430), which at a later time greatly influenced the Church's teaching on the minister of the sacraments.[8] St. Augustine stated that the worthiness or unworthiness of the minister did not affect the validity of baptism. It was Christ who baptized, and his baptism could be effected through the instrumentality of Judas or John. It was not a question of who instrumentally administered the baptism, but of what was administered in the ceremony of baptism.[9]

In the thirteenth century St. Thomas Aquinas (ca. 1225-1274) taught that the previous reception of baptism was necessary in order that a person might validly receive confirmation. He stated that the sacramental character of confirmation presupposed the

---

[5] Cf. pp. 8-9 of this dissertation.

[6] Cf. S. Stephen I (254-257), *Epistola ad Cyprianum* (74)—Denzinger, *Enchiridion,* nn. 46-47, and appended footnotes; Council of Arles (314), canon 8—Mansi, II, 472.

[7] Cf. Conc. Trident., sess. VII, *de sacramento baptismi,* canon 4: "Si quis dixerit baptismum qui etiam datur ab haereticis in nomine Patris et Filii et Spiritus Sancti, cum intentione faciendi quod facit Ecclesia, non esse verum baptismum": A. S.—Denzinger, *Enchiridion,* n. 860.

[8] Cf. Tanquerey, *Synopsis Theologiae Dogmaticae* (24. ed., 3 vols., Parisiis-Tornaci-Romae: Desclée et Socii, 1938), III, n. 409 (to be referred to hereafter as *Synopsis*).

[9] *Contra Cresconium Donatistam,* lib. III, cap. 6—*CSEL,* LII, 415. Cf. Waldron, *The Minister of Baptism,* The Catholic University of America Canon Law Studies, n. 170 (Washington, D. C.: The Catholic University of America Press, 1942), pp. 22-24.

presence in the soul of the character of baptism; that the relation of confirmation to baptism was like that of growth to generation. Just as one not yet born cannot advance to maturity, so until one is first baptized he cannot receive confirmation.[10] Consequently, should an unbaptized person be administered confirmation, he would not receive anything, and would have to be again confirmed after the reception of valid baptism.[11]

This doctrine of St. Thomas was accorded the full approval of theologians and represents their common teaching on the subject.

A second condition requisite for the valid reception of confirmation is required in the case of adults, and that is the presence of a due intention.[12] Since, however, this factor has no history with particular reference to confirmation, it will be given consideration only in the doctrinal section of this dissertation.

ARTICLE 2. FOR THE LICIT AND FRUITFUL RECEPTION OF THE SACRAMENT

Since confirmation is a sacrament of the living, the state of grace is required for its lawful and fruitful reception.[13] When baptism and confirmation were administered together, the state of grace was achieved through the reception of baptism.[14] When the two sacraments were administered on different occasions the problem would be present as to how the state of grace was to be realized in those adults who had committed serious sins since their reception of baptism. Would the confession of these sins be necessary before approaching confirmation, or would an act of perfect contrition which included a desire for the sacrament of penance be sufficient?[15]

As early as 858 there appeared in the *Diocesan Capitula* compiled by Herardus, Archbishop of Tours, the canon that all who are old enough should come fasting to receive confirmation, and

---

[10] *Summa Theologica,* Pars III, q. 72, a. 6.

[11] St. Thomas, *loc. cit.*

[12] Coronata, I, n. 89.

[13] Cf. Coronata, I, n. 172.

[14] Cf. Coronata, I, n. 104.

[15] Cf. Tanquerey, *Synopsis,* III, n. 751.

should be admonished to confess their sins beforehand in order that, cleansed from them, they might be found worthy to receive the Holy Ghost.[16]

In 1280 when the Fathers of the Council of Cologne stated that children were not to be admitted to confirmation until the age of seven, they specified at the same time that if the recipients were ten years or more of age they were to confess their sins to the priest before receiving the sacrament.[17] Seven years later the Council of Exeter made confession of sins obligatory on the part of all adult recipients on the day on which they were to be confirmed.[18]

In 1536, sacramental confession was placed before the people in the form of a recommendation by the Council of Cologne as a means of preparing for a worthy reception of the sacrament.[19] Before the end of the sixteenth century, however, many councils were not content with merely recommending sacramental confession as a means of disposing oneself for a worthy reception of confirmation, but made this condition a matter of obligation.[20]

The Council of Bordeaux (1583) was less strict in its ordinance regarding the requirement of previous confession; it suggested as an alternative "at least a great sorrow for sins and a firm purpose of approaching the tribunal of penance."[21]

The Catechism issued in connection with the Council of Trent did not affirm the necessity of confession prior to the reception of

---

[16] *Capitula Herardi,* canon 75—*MPL,* CXXI, 769; Burchard, *Decretum,* lib. IV, canon 60—*MPL,* CXL, 738; Ivo, *Panormia,* lib. I, cap. 119—*MPL,* CLXI, 1071.

[17] Canon 5—Mansi, XXIV, 349.

[18] Canon 3—Mansi, XXIV, 787.

[19] Pars septima, canon 9—Mansi, XXXIII, 1258.

[20] Council of Besançon (1571), canon 3—Mansi, XXXVI bis, 52; IV Council of Milan (1576), pars II, cap. 3—Mansi, XXXIV A, 221; Council of Rouen (1581), *De Sacr. Conf.*—Mansi, XXXIV A, 623-624; Council of Rheims (1583), cap. 9—Mansi, XXXIV A, 690; Council of Bourges (1584), canon 6—Mansi, XXXIV A, 889; Council of Aix (1585), *De Conf. Sacr.*—Mansi, XXXIV B, 946-947.

[21] Cap. 9: "Qui adulti sunt ut ad tantum sacramentum non accedant nisi praemissa peccatorum confessione, aut saltem maximo peccatorum dolore et mature confitendi proposito."—Mansi, XXXIV A, 690.

confirmation. It stated that adults who desired to receive worthily had to bring with them faith and piety. But this alone did not suffice. They were also to grieve from their hearts for their more weighty sins. As to sacramental confession, it was stated only that the pastor was to exhort the prospective recipients to confess their sins.[22] Moreover, it was the opinion of Suarez (1548-1617) that, if a person was aware of the guilt of a serious sin before receiving confirmation, he could not be obliged strictly to seek a sacramental absolution as the one means for its forgiveness.[23]

Nevertheless in the eighteenth and nineteenth centuries laws requiring that confirmation be preceded by sacramental confession appeared among the statutes of many particular councils.[24]

The Council of New Granada (1868), without however insisting upon the necessity of previous confession, called upon pastors to teach the people that confirmation was a sacrament of the living, and that consequently it was necessary for the recipient not to be tainted with any guilt of grievous sin, if he is to experience a licit and fruitful reception; otherwise, although he would receive the sacramental character, he would not acquire the sanctifying grace. Moreover, he would commit a new and more grievous sin, and at the same time be guilty of sacrilege.[25]

Two documents of the Holy See which dealt with the question of confirmation and previous confession did not indicate definitely that confession must precede the reception of confirmation.

---

[22] *Catechism of the Council of Trent,* pp. 183-184.

[23] *De Sacramento Confirmationis,* q. 72, art. 7, sec. 2, n. 7—*Opera Omnia* (26 vols., Parisiis, 1856-1861), XX, 665 (henceforth to be referred to with the name of the author).

[24] Council of Fermo (1726), Tit. XV—Mansi, XXXVII, 638; Council of Avignon (1849), Tit. IV, cap. 3—*Coll. Lac.,* IV, 337; Council of Rheims (1849), Tit. VI, cap. 2—*Coll. Lac.,* IV, 115; Council of Auch (1850), Tit. III, cap. 1, pars 2, canon 78—*Coll. Lac.,* IV, 1185; Council of Cashel (1853), Tit. III—*Coll. Lac.,* III, 833; Council of Vienna (1858), Tit. III, cap. 3—*Coll. Lac.,* V, 162.

[25] Tit. IV, cap. III: "Parochi . . . insinuant imprimis confirmationem esse sacramentum vivorum, ac proinde ad eam licite et cum fructu suscipiendam necesse esse ut illam suscepturus nulla lethalis culpae sorde sit inquinatus; secus enim characterem quidem, non vero gratiam sanctificationem reciperet, immo novam graviorem culpam admitteret et fieret sacrilegii reus."—*Coll. Lac.,* VI, 502.

The Sacred Congregation for the Propagation of the Faith stated that in order that those who have the use of reason may receive the sacrament worthily, it is incumbent on them to be in the state of grace, and accordingly it is most fitting that they previously make a sacramental confession.[26]

A reply of the Holy Office stated that the practice of taking care that adults confess their sins before receiving confirmation was very much in keeping with the practice dictated by the Roman Pontifical.[27]

Apparently the "taking care that adults confess their sins" was understood by the Holy Office to refer to a persuading or exhorting of the people to go to confession, because the Roman Pontifical gives the recipients the choice of either confessing their sins, or of at least being sorry for their mortal sins if they have been committed.[28]

A second requirement for the licit and fruitful reception of confirmation is the acquisition of sufficient instruction.

During the time when the reception of confirmation constituted a part of the rite of initiation into the Church, there was an elaborate preparation by way of instruction in Christian doctrine, so that adult recipients would approach the rites with the possession of a commensurate knowledge of religious truth.[29] However, when confirmation came to be administered apart from baptism, so that its reception had to await the age of discretion, there does not seem to be any evidence that a specific degree of religious information was required of the subject for the licit reception of this sacrament, until the sixteenth century.[30]

In 1536 the Council of Cologne spoke of an instruction in con-

---

[26] Instr. 4 maii 1774—*Fontes,* n. 4565.

[27] (Vic. Ap. Sandwic.) 11 dec. 1850: 15. "Nous avons soin que les adultes se confessent avant de recevoir cet auguste Sacrament."

Ad 15. "Hanc praxim esse apprime conformem praxi imperatae § 4 Romani Pontificalis, *De Confirmatione,* ideoque laudandam."—*Fontes,* n. 913.

[28] *Pontificale Romanum* (Mechliniae, 1845) Pars Prima, *De Confirmandis:* "Adulti deberent prius peccata confiteri et postea confirmari vel saltem de mortalibus si in ea inciderint conterantur."

[29] Cf. Martène, *De Antiquis Ecclesiae Ritibus* (3 vols., Rotomagi, 1700), I, 26-28 (henceforth to be referred to with the name of the author).

[30] Cf. Martène, I, 238.

nection with the reception of the sacrament. In the course of questioning the propriety of bestowing the sacrament upon infants, this council leaned to the view that confirmation should not be administered to infants, but that it should be deferred until a later date, when the recipient might profit by a timely instruction.[31]

The IV Council of Milan (1576), seeing the need of some instruction for the worthy reception of the sacrament, recommended that urban pastors, and also others who in the cities were charged with the care of souls, teach the people with what great zeal they should receive confirmation.[32]

The V Council of Milan (1579) was among the first to exact a manifestation of religious knowledge on the part of the recipient. This council stated that persons among the classes and masses of the unlettered were to be required to know at least the Lord's Prayer, the Angelical Salutation and the Apostles' Creed.[33] Of other councils of this century two of them demanded only a knowledge of the Apostles' Creed.[34] The Council of Rheims (1583) demanded a knowledge of the Lord's Prayer in addition to that of the Apostles' Creed.[35]

The Council of Aix (1585) was somewhat more exacting than the other councils of the sixteenth century as to the degree of knowledge which the recipient of confirmation had to possess. This council stated that the subject's knowledge of his religion had to be manifested at least through his ability to recite the Lord's Prayer, the Hail Mary, the Apostles' Creed and the Ten Commandments.[36]

The Catechism of the Council of Trent indicated the desirability of having the prospective recipients understand the meaning and effects of confirmation. The Catechism stated that if ever the diligence of pastors was required in explaining the sacrament of confirmation that time existed then, "when this sacrament is altogether omitted by many in the holy Church of God, whilst there

---

[31] Pars septima, canon 9—Mansi, XXXII, 1258.

[32] Pars II, cap. 3—Mansi, XXXIV A, 221.

[33] Pars I, cap. 8—Mansi, XXXIV A, 363.

[34] Council of Rouen (1581), *De Sacr. Conf.*—Mansi, XXXIV A, 623-624; Council of Bourges (1584), Tit. XX, canon 4—Mansi, XXXIV A, 899.

[35] Cap. 9—Mansi, XXXIV A, 690.

[36] *De Conf. Sacr.*—Mansi, XXXIV B, 946-947.

are very few who study to derive therefrom the fruit of grace which they ought."[37]

In 1639 the Council of Benevento recommended that children should not be admitted to confirmation until they had attained the age of seven years and had moreover acquired a substantial knowledge of the rudiments of the faith. Furthermore, this council inculcated that it was the duty of pastors so to admonish their parishioners regarding the nature, the dignity and the efficacy of this sacrament, that their people would know not only that the sacrament should not be neglected, but also that it should be received with the greatest piety and fervor, lest through their own fault this divine benefit be conferred upon them in vain.[38]

In the following century a basis for determining the degree of knowledge of Christian doctrine which should be required of a candidate for confirmation was furnished by the Encyclical *Etsi minime* of Pope Benedict XIV.[39] This letter stated that bishops should warn pastors not to furnish testimonials for the reception of confirmation to those who are ignorant of the more important questions of faith and doctrine and who lack knowledge regarding the power and efficacy of the sacrament.

In the nineteenth century the Council of Prague (1860) decreed that those who awaited confirmation were to be instructed as to the nature and dignity of confirmation, and moreover they were to be examined on their knowledge of the fundamental prayers, the rudiments of the faith and the commandments of God and of the Church.[40] Other councils of this century, while not as explicit in their demands as the Council of Prague, nevertheless provided that candidates be sufficiently instructed before they be allowed to receive confirmation.[41]

---

[37] P. 175.

[38] Tit. XXXVI, canons 10, 12—Mansi, XXXVI ter, 585-586.

[39] 7 febr. 1742, § 9—*Fontes,* n. 324.

[40] Tit. IV, cap. 3—*Coll. Lac.,* V, 493.

[41] Council of Avignon (1849), Tit. IV, cap. III—*Coll. Lac.,* IV, 337; Council of Toulouse (1850), Tit. III, cap. I—*Coll. Lac.,* IV, 1053; Council of Auch (1850), Tit. III, cap. 1, pars 2, canon 77—*Coll. Lac.,* IV, 1185; Council of Bordeaux (1850), Tit. III, cap. 3—*Coll. Lac.,* IV, 568; Council of Cashel (1853), Tit. III, *Coll. Lac.,* III, 833; Council of Quebec (1854), decr. VIII—*Coll. Lac.,* III, 635; Council of Vienna (1858), Tit. III, cap. 3—*Coll. Lac.,* V, 162.

The question regarding the requisite knowledge of Christian doctine for the reception of confirmation was involved in a reply of the Holy See which had to do with infirm adults who were unable to come to church. In that reply it was stated that confirmation was not to be given to those among them whom the missionaries thought entitled to receive baptism when they were at the point of death, unless these persons had at least some intention of receiving confirmation as a source and means of strength for their souls. But such adults upon their recovery were diligently to be taught the mysteries of their faith and the nature of the sacraments received by them.[42]

ARTICLE 3. FOR COMPLIANCE WITH THE RITUALISTIC REQUIREMENTS

A number of councils around the middle of the nineteenth century included in their decrees the rule that all recipients were to be present at the beginning of the ceremony, and were not to leave until after the benediction given by the bishop at the end of the ceremony.[43]

This particular point was given further development when the Holy Office was called on to respond to the question whether a child was to be considered confirmed although it was not present at the first imposition of the bishop's hands, since repeatedly it happens, especially when there is a great number of children to receive confirmation, that some child will mingle with the group of the recipients even though it was not present at the first imposition of hands. The answer to the query was given in the affirmative, but an insistence on the proper care that all be present at the first imposition of hands accompanied this affirmative reply.[44]

A ritualistic requirement which has its roots in ancient tradition is the use of a sponsor at confirmation. The liturgy of the early

---

[42] S.C.S. Off. (Tchely Meridio-Oriental), 10 apr. 1861—*Fontes,* n. 965.

[43] Council of Cashel (1853), Tit. III, n. 4—*Coll. Lac.,* III, 833; Council of Quebec (1854), Decr. VIII, n. 3—*Coll. Lac.,* III, 635; Council of Prague (1860), Tit. IV, cap. 3—*Coll. Lac.,* V, 493.

[44] S.C.S. Off. (Aretin.), 17 apr. 1872—*Fontes,* n. 1022.

Church demanded that a sponsor be employed during the rites of initiation of which confirmation formed a part.[45]

Moreover there is evidence of a time as early as 756 to show that a sponsor was used for the ceremony of confirmation, when that sacrament was conferred apart from the administration of baptism.[46] This evidence is to be found in a canon of the Council of Compiègne (756), which stated that if anyone acted as godparent for his own child while the bishop administered confirmation, that person was to be separated from his spouse and was not to marry another.[47]

Apparently the same law was in force in Chalon-sur-Saône, for a canon of a council that was held there reports that some women fraudulently acted as godmothers for their own children in order to effect a legal separation from their husband. The Fathers of the Council of Chalon-sur-Saône (813) decided to eradicate this abuse, and accordingly condemned such women to perpetual penance, while at the same time it decreed that they were not to be separated from their husbands.[48]

There is no indication in the decrees of the Councils either of Compiègne or of Chalon-sur-Saône that the practice of having a sponsor at confirmation was something of recent origin. Hence there seems to be no reason for disclaiming the belief that godparents had been employed in this sacrament from the time that its conferral first became separated from the rite of baptism.[49]

The use of a sponsor at confirmation was attested by the Coun-

---

[45] Cf. Martène, I, 153.

[46] Villien, pp. 81-82.

[47] Canon XII: "Si quis filiastrum aut filiastram ante episcopum ad confirmationem tenuerit, separetur ab uxore sua et alteram non accipiat."—Hardouin, *Acta Conciliorum et Epistolae Decretales ac Constitutiones Summorum Pontificum* (12 vols., Parisiis, 1714-1715), III, 2005 (to be cited henceforth as Hardouin).

[48] Canon XXXI: "Dictum est nobis quasdam feminas desidiose, quasdam vero fraudulenter, ut a viris suis separentur proprios filios coram episcopis ad confirmandum tenuisse. Unde nos dignum duximus, ut, si qua mulier filium suum desidia aut fraude aliqua coram episcopo ad confirmandum tenuerit propter fallaciam suam, penitentiam agat; a viro tamen suo non separetur."—Hardouin, V, 1036.

[49] Cf. Villien, p. 82.

cil of London in 1200 when the Fathers of that council declared that mothers, fathers, stepmothers and stepfathers were not eligible to act as godparents for their own children.[50]

In the same century the rôle of the sponsor in confirmation was elaborated upon by St. Thomas. He explained that confirmation was given to man as a source of strength in the spiritual struggle, and just as one newly born needed someone to teach him in matters which pertained to ordinary conduct, so those who were being readied for battle had need of instructors who could inform them of the things which concerned the conduct of the battle. So it was that, in earthly wars, generals and captains were appointed to command others. Wherefore, one who received this sacrament had another person to stand for him, who, as it were, had the duty of instructing him concerning the spiritual combat. Similarly, since this sacrament conferred upon the recipient the perfection of maturity, the one who approached confirmation is upheld by another in that he was spiritually a weakling and a child.[51]

The question of the obligation to have a sponsor at confirmation was also contemplated by St. Alphonsus (1696-1787). He affirmed the existence of this obligation and stated that it was gravely binding in cases wherein a sponsor could be obtained.[52] This opinion of St. Alphonsus was made the basis of a decision by the Holy Office, in which this Congregation refused to a bishop a general faculty that would have authorized him to dispense with sponsors at confirmation.[53]

The duty of employing godparents at confirmation was further specified by a rubric of the Roman Pontifical which forbade that one person should act as godparent for more than one or at most two candidates for confirmation, unless in the judgment of the bishop the factor of necessity dictated otherwise.[54]

[50] Decretum III: ". . . Adicimus etiam ut nullus teneatur ad confirmationem a patre, vel matre, vel vitrico, vel noverca. . . ."—Mansi, XXII, 714.

[51] *Summa Theologica,* Pars III, q. 72, a. 10; cf. Sainte-Beuve, *Tractatus de Sacramentis Confirmationis et Unctionis Extremae* (Parisiis, 1686), p. 337 (henceforth to be referred to with the name of the author).

[52] *Theologia Moralis,* lib. VI, n. 185.

[53] Instr. (ad Archiep. Portus Principis), 5 sept. 1877—*Fontes,* n. 1053.

[54] *Pontificale Romanum,* Pars Prima, *De Confirmandis:* "Nullus praesentet nisi unum, aut duos, non plures, nisi aliter necessitas suadeat, arbitrio Episcopi."

This rule of the Pontifical formed part of a decree of the II Plenary Council of Baltimore (1866). In calling upon bishops to leave no stone unturned that the approved discipline of employing sponsors at confirmation be introduced in the dioceses where it did not already obtain, the Fathers of this Council stated that each person being confirmed was to have an individual sponsor, and that men were not to perform this function for women who were being confirmed, nor were women to act as sponsors for the men. The fathers further stated that should this law be altogether impossible of observance, then at least two men should be used to act as sponsors for the boys, and two women for the girls.[55]

The Holy Office in a letter to the Bishop of Burlington, reaffirmed the fact that this custom, tolerated by the Council of Baltimore, was allowable only in cases of necessity.[56]

---

[55] "Quanquam de necessitate hujus sacramenti non sit, ut in eo recipiendo Patrinus vel Matrina adhibeatur, cum tamen id laudabilis Ecclesiae consuetudo suadeat, sacrique canones praescribant, Episcopi nullum non movebunt lapidem, ut disciplina hujusmodi, jam in nonnullis harum Provinciarum Dioecesibus invecta, ubique introducatur. Confirmati vero habebunt Patrinos singuli singulos, nec tamen foeminis mares nec maribus foeminae Patrini officium praestabunt. Quod si hoc fieri omnino nequeat, saltem duo pro pueris Patrini, et duae pro puellis Matrinae adhibeantur."—*Concilii Plenarii Baltimorensis II Acta et Decreta* (Baltimorae: Joannes Murphy, 1868), n. 253.

[56] 26 nov. 1873—*Collectanea S. C. de Prop. Fide,* II, n. 1408; *Fontes,* n. 1027.

CHAPTER V

Conditions Required with Reference to the Time and Place of Confirmation

ARTICLE 1. THE TIME FOR THE CONFERRING OF CONFIRMATION

Relative to the indicated time for the conferring of confirmation it is necessary to distinguish between the administration of confirmation along with that of baptism as part of the rite of initiation, and the conferring of confirmation by itself, apart from baptism. In the former instance the days that were first designated for the solemn ceremony of initiation were the vigils of Easter and Pentecost.[1] The day that was given preference was the vigil of Easter. If, however, the neophyte had not yet given sufficient proof of his worthiness, or if for any reason he could not present himself for the rite of initiation on that day, the ceremony was deferred until a later day in Eastertime, and the final day for this purpose was the vigil of Pentecost.[2]

The popes and councils restricted the conferral of baptism to this period. They forbade its administration outside the solemnities of Easter and Pentecost, except in case of necessity.[3]

In the East, the feast of the Epiphany, commemorative of the birth of Christ and also of the day on which he received the bap-

---

[1] Cf. Martène, I, 2; Duchesne, p. 293.

[2] Duchesne, *loc. cit.*

[3] Cf. Siricius (384-398), *Epistola ad Himerium ep. Tarraconensem,* 10 febr. 385—Jaffé, *Regesta,* n. 255; Leo I (440-461), *Epistola,* 20 oct. 414—Jaffé, *Regesta,* n. 414; Council of Gerona (517), canon IV: "De catechumenis baptizandis id statutum est ut in paschae solemnitate vel pentecostes, quanto maioris celebritatis maior celebritas est, tanto magis ad baptizandum veniant: ceteris solemnitatibus infirmi tantummodo debeant baptizari: quibus quocunque tempore convenit baptismum non negari."—Hardouin, II, 1043-1044; cf. also Council of Auxerre (578), canon 18—Mansi, IX, 913-914; II Council of Mâcon (585), canon 3—Mansi, IX, 951; Council of Mayence (813), canon 4—Hardouin, IV, 1010; Council of Rouen (1072), canon 24—Hardouin, VI A, 1192.

tism of St. John, was added to the days on which the ceremonies of initiation could be held.[4] The example of the East was followed by some of the churches of the West, and in addition there arose the custom of including Christmas and several other feasts among the days for the conferring of the rites of initiation.[5] However, the popes insisted that the Latin churches observe the custom of confining the administration of these rites to the solemnities of Easter and Pentecost.[6]

It evidently became the custom after the fourth century in the rural churches in the West to confer confirmation separately from the administration of baptism.[7] This was necessitated by the fact that the rural churches were some distance removed from the city of the bishop's residence, so that the full rites of initiation could not conveniently be held on the one occasion.[8]

St. Jerome (342-420) furnished testimony which at least suggested that when this development took place there was no specified time for the conferral of confirmation alone. From his testimony it seems that, after baptism had been given by a priest or a deacon, the time for bestowing confirmation became contingent upon the bishop's opportunity to visit the rural district.[9] The text in the writings of St. Jerome treated of the custom of the churches according to which the bishops went out to the distant small towns and there imposed hands on those who had previously been baptized by priests or deacons.[10]

A further indication that in the early Church the time for conferring confirmation apart from baptism was left to the discretion of the bishop is to be found in canon 4 of the Council of Soissons (744), which called upon abbots and priests to be of assistance to

---

[4] Martène, I, 3; Duchesne, pp. 293-294; Sainte-Beuve, p. 340.

[5] Martène, I, 3-5; Duchesne, *loc. cit.;* Mourret-Thompson, I, 535-536.

[6] Cf. Leo I, *Epistola,* 20 oct. 414—Jaffé, *Regesta,* n. 414; Duchesne, p. 294.

[7] Reichel, p. 51; Mourret-Thompson, III, 221.

[8] Cf. Martène, I, 234.

[9] Cf. Sainte-Beuve, p. 340; Martène, I, 234.

[10] *Dialogus adversus Luciferanos:* "Non quidem abnuo hanc esse Ecclesiarum consuetudinem, ut ad eos qui longe a maioribus urbibus per presbyteros et diacanos baptizati sunt, episcopus ad invocationem sancti Spiritus manum impositurus excurrat."—*MPL,* XXIII, 164; cf. Martène, *loc. cit.*

the bishop on the occasion of his canonical visit to the parish to provide the people with confirmation.[11]

The same arrangement regarding the time for the administering of confirmation was confirmed by the Council of Bordeaux in 1262. This Council provided that when the bishop visits his diocese, the pastor, having previously received word of his coming, should advise his subjects, so that they may prepare themselves for the reception of this sacrament.[12]

The examples seen thus far as reflecting the practice of administering confirmation outside the times reserved for the ceremonies of initiation were cases wherein this arrangement was necessary for the reason that no bishop was present on the occasion of baptism to complete the solemn rites with the conferral of confirmation. However, even in the larger cities, where this reason did not obtain, there came into evidence around the ninth century some exceptions to the traditional custom of bestowing baptism and confirmation together, although the practice of conferring baptism and confirmation together on the same occasion prevailed for the most part up to the thirteenth century.[13] Accounting for these exceptions was the fact that in some instances the numbers of those to be baptized and confirmed had increased to such an extent that both sacraments could not conveniently be administered on the one occasion.[14]

What is perhaps a reflection of this situation and one of the initial departures from the tradition maintained in the larger cities, namely, of restricting the conferral of confirmation to set periods of time, is a famous decree of the Council of Paris (829), which urged the administration of confirmation to the infirm and the dying. This decree stated that as in the two seasons of Easter and Pentecost, both baptism and confirmation are conferred, so also not only the grace of baptism should be hastened for the sick

---

[11] ". . . et quando iure canonico episcopus circumit parochiam ad confirmandum populum, abbates et presbyteri parati sint ad suscipiendum episcopum in adiutorium necessitatis."—Hardouin, III, 1033; cf. also Council of Chalon-sur-Saône (813), canon 14—Hardouin, IV, 1034.

[12] Canon 4—Hardouin, VII, 553-554.

[13] Cf. Martène, I, 234.

[14] Martène, *loc. cit.*

and dying, but also the gift of the Holy Ghost should be accorded to them without delay.[15]

In the face of the moral impossibility of accommodating the large numbers of the faithful on single days with respect to both baptism and confirmation, there arose the usage of setting aside certain days for the reception of the latter sacrament alone.[16] In some localities the octave of the day of one's baptism came to be designated as the day for the reception of confirmation.[17] The time recommended by Amalarius (+ 815) was the third hour of the feast of Pentecost itself, in order that thus there might be fittingly commemorated the day and the hour in which the Holy Ghost desended upon the apostles.[18] The Ambrosian ceremonial, which possibly dates back to the tenth century,[19] called for the conferral of confirmation five days after the feast of Easter.[20]

From the thirteenth century onward, when the deferral of confirmation until the subject had acquired the use of reason came to be the almost universal practice, until the sixteenth century, many councils established laws with regard to the administration and reception of confirmation, but did not impose any restriction as to the time for its bestowal.[21] However, the factor which was prob-

---

[15] Pars I, canon 33: "Sicut autem duobus temporibus, Pascha videlicet et Pentecoste, baptismus; ita etiam traditio sancti Spiritus per impositionem manuum fidelibus tradatur; exceptis videlicet ut dictum est infirmis et morte periclitantibus: quibus sicut baptismatis gratia succurrendum, ita incunctanter donum Spiritus sancti est tradendum."—Hardouin, IV, 1318.

[16] Cf. Martène, I, 234-236.

[17] Cf. Alcuin (+ 804), *De Divinis Officiis,* cap. VIII—*MPL,* CI, 1183; Rabanus (+ 856), *De Institutione Clericorum,* lib. II, cap. 39—*MPL,* CVII, 352.

[18] *De Ecclesiasticis Officiis Libri Quatuor,* lib. IV, cap. 29—*MPL,* CV, 1217; cf. Acts, II, 1-16.

[19] Cf. Duchesne, p. 160.

[20] Cf. Martène, I, 235.

[21] Cf. Council of Cologne (1280), canon 3—Mansi, XXIII, 1004; Council of Avignon (1457), canons 14, 15—Mansi, XXXII, 187; Council of Cologne (1536), pars septima, canons 8-13—Mansi, XXXII, 1258; Council of Capua (1569), *De Confirmatione*—Mansi, XXXV A, 710; Council of Besançon (1571), canons 1-8—Mansi, XXXVI bis, 52; Council of Rouen (1581), *De Sacr. Conf.*—Mansi, XXXIV A, 623-624; Council of Rheims (1583), cap. 9—Mansi, XXXIV A, 690; Council of Bordeaux (1583), cap. 10—Mansi, XXXIV A, 756.

ably at least partly responsible for this circumstance was the fact that during this period the reception of confirmation had become subject to considerable neglect on the part of the people.[22] Hence the Fathers of these councils were chiefly concerned with securing a more widespread and more worthy reception of the sacrament. The time for its conferral was apparently left to the bishop's opportunity and discretion.[23] Nevertheless, among the councils of the sixteenth century there were several which specified the times during which confirmation was to be administered.

The IV Council of Milan (1576) ordered that the sacrament be given during the solemnities of Pentecost and at the time of the bishop's visitation of his diocese.[24] The V Council of Milan (1579) looked upon the third hour of the day which commemorated the feast of Pentecost as the time most fitting for the conferral of confirmation. However, the bestowal of the sacrament was not to be limited to this occasion, so that, if the number of recipients was sufficiently great, then it should be given also at Easter time, during Advent and throughout the course of the bishop's visitation.[25]

The Council of Bourges (1584) provided that the sacrament be administered during the weeks of the Ember days.[26] In a more specific way the Council of Aix (1585) indicated a preference for the third hour on the day of the solemnities of Pentecost as the most appropriate time for this function.[27] It is evident from the texts of several of these councils that the fittingness of the third hour of the feast of Pentecost for providing the faithful with confirmation, which had been noted by Amalarius[28] in the early ninth century, had come to be recognized.

The Catechism of the Council of Trent stated that confirmation was to be administered principally at Pentecost, for it was on that day that the Apostles were strengthened by the Holy Ghost. The recollection of this event should serve for the recipient's realization

---

[22] Cf. *Catechism of the Council of Trent,* p. 175.
[23] Cf. Sainte-Beuve, p. 340.
[24] Pars II, cap. 3—Mansi, XXXIV A, 221.
[25] Pars I, cap. 8—Mansi, XXXIV A, 363.
[26] Canon 7—Mansi, XXXIV A, 899.
[27] *De Conf. Sacr.*—Mansi, XXXIV B, 946-947.
[28] *De Ecclesiasticis Officiis Libri Quatuor,* lib. IV, cap. 29—*MPL,* CV, 1217.

and appreciation with reference to the greatness of the mysteries stored up within the sacrament.[29]

In the eighteenth century a similar statement was issued as part of an Instruction of the Sacred Congregation for the Propagation of the Faith. It was stated by this Sacred Congregation that, although confirmation may be administered at any time, it is particularly fitting that it be given in Pentecost week and at about the third hour, the time in which the Holy Ghost descended upon the Apostles.[30]

During the nineteenth century the time for the administration of confirmation was in most places apparently considered entirely a matter to be determined by the bishop. This conclusion may be derived through an inspection of the decrees of the various councils of that century which, while they promulgated laws regarding the reception of confirmation, did not enact any regulations regarding the time in which the sacrament was to be conferred.[31]

ARTICLE 2. THE PLACE FOR THE CONFERRING OF CONFIRMATION

Relative to the history of the requisite place for the reception of confirmation a distinction must be made between the earliest stages of the Church's development, when as yet there were not in existence any churches or oratories as these are now understood, and the later stages, when the Church had erected edifices for the public worship of the faithful.

In the former case it seems that the scene of confirmation was whatever locality had been chosen for the assembly of the faithful.[32]

---

[29] P. 186.

[30] Instr., 4 maii 1774—*Fontes,* n. 4565.

[31] Cf. Council of Tours (1849), Decr. VII—*Coll. Lac.,* IV, 275; Council of Sens (1850), Tit. III, cap. 4—*Coll. Lac.,* IV, 889; Council of Auch (1850), Tit. III, cap. 1—*Coll. Lac.,* IV, 1185; Council of Rouen (1850), Decr. XIV—*Coll. Lac.,* IV, 528; Council of Toulouse (1850), Tit. III, cap 1 —*Coll. Lac.,* IV, 1053; Council of Bordeaux (1850), Tit. III, cap. 3—*Coll. Lac.,* IV, 568; Council of Cashel (1853), Tit. III—*Coll. Lac.,* III, 833; Council of Quebec (1854), Decr. VIII—*Coll. Lac.,* III, 635; II Plenary Council of Baltimore (1866), Tit. IV, cap. 3—*Coll. Lac.,* III, 462-463; Council of Vienna (1858), Tit. III, cap. 3—*Coll. Lac.,* V, 162; Council of Prague (1860), Tit. IV, cap. 3—*Coll. Lac.,* V, 493.

[32] Cf. Mourret-Thompson, I, 282-283.

For after the catechumen had received baptism, the scene of which was generally some river or pool of water,[33] he was clothed in a white garment and introduced into the assembly of the faithful, where the bishop by means of the imposition of hands and the anointing with chrism conferred upon him the sacrament of confirmation.[34]

After the Church's material advancement had reached the stage at which it had come into the possession and use of churches, a further distinction obtained. Relative to this period one must distinguish between the faithful in the larger cities, where up to the thirteenth century and as a general rule confirmation was conferred immediatedy after baptism,[35] and the Christians of the rural areas, where from the fourth or fifth century baptism and confirmation came to be administered separately.[36]

In the former instance the church or chapel was the place prescribed by the liturgical books for the rites of initiation, which consisted of the reception of baptism, of confirmation and of the Holy Eucharist.[37] For a time the performance of these rites was restricted to the cathedral church in the city of the bishop's residence, inasmuch as for some time only the bishops ordinarily administered baptism, and hence baptistries existed only at their churches.[38]

In some of the churches wherein the rites of initiation were held there had been erected a special chapel, called the *consignatorium,* which was set apart for the administration of confirmation.[39] Moreover, when a church had become the place where confirmation was received under normal circumstances, it was naturally to be assumed in the absence of any evident reason to the contrary that it was in a church that the status of the faithful as Chris-

---

[33] Cf. Martène, I, 7-8.

[34] Cf. Tertullian (ca. 160-ca. 230), *Liber de Baptismo,* cap. VII-VIII—*CSEL,* XX, 207; Mourret-Thompson, *loc. cit.*

[35] Cf. Martène, I, 234.

[36] Cf. Reichel, p. 51; Sainte-Beuve, pp. 340-341.

[37] Cf. *Ordo Romanus I*—Mabillon, *Museum Italicum,* II, 27; Duchesne, p. 314; Martène, I, 240.

[38] Martène, I, 12.

[39] This chapel was so called because confirmation was frequently referred to as the "*consignatio*" (sealing). Cf. Martène, I, 240; Duchesne, p. 314; Reichel, p. 51.

tians was perfected, not only when they had received their baptism in serious illness, but also when they had become converted from some heretical sect.[40]

It was around the fourth or fifth century that churches of the towns and villages evidently began to be the scene of the administration of confirmation apart from baptism.[41] While the text of St. Jerome (342-420) in which he acknowledged the custom of the churches in accordance with which the bishop went out to the distant smaller towns to confirm those who had been baptized by the priest or deacons,[42] does not specifically certify that the churches themselves were the scene of confirmation, it seems most likely that such was the case.[43] If churches existed in the rural areas, they constituted the obvious places for the conferral of confirmation, and the presence in such communities of the priests and the deacons who had previously given baptism seems plainly to point to the existence of churches to which these ministers were attached.

Although a church or a chapel was the normal place in the larger cities for the conferral of confirmation, and probably also in the smaller towns, yet, according to a canon contained in the works of medieval compilers and attributed by them to a Council of Rheims, a wider latitude was conceded to the bishop when circumstances required it. This canon stated that a bishop was permitted to confirm on the battlefield in a case of necessity.[44]

Inasmuch as an investigation of the texts of the councils held at Rheims has failed to disclose this canon, it cannot be stated with certainty that the decree is genuine, or, if geunine, what degree of antiquity it possesses. Nevertheless, the Council of Paris (829) contains a canon which urged the conferral of confirmation to those who were ill or in danger of death, which of necessity called for

---

[40] Cf. Leo I (440-461), *Epistola ad Nicetam*—Jaffé, *Regesta,* n. 563; Council of Elvira (ca. 306), canon 38—Mansi, II, 12; Council of Arles (314), canon 6—Mansi, II, 471.

[41] Cf. Sainte-Beuve, pp. 340-341; Reichel, *loc. cit.*

[42] *Dialogus adversus Luciferanos*—*MPL,* XXIII, 164.

[43] Cf. Sainte-Beuve, p. 341.

[44] Burchard, *Decretum,* lib. IV, cap. 68—*MPL,* CXL, 740; Ivo, *Decretum,* pars I, cap. 262—*MPL,* CXLI, 121.

an administration of the sacrament in a place other than a church or a chapel.[45] A similar plea was later made by the V Council of Milan (1579).[46]

The Instruction of the Sacred Congregation for the Propagation of the Faith, dated May 4, 1774, stated that confirmation could be conferred less solemnly and even privately in homes, or outside any church or oratory, to sick children, or even to adults who for any legitimate reason could not come to the church.[47] A similar provision is contained in a rubric of the Roman Pontifical, which conceded to the bishop the right to decide when circumstances warranted a less solemn administration of confirmation in a place other than a church or an oratory.[48]

During the sixteenth century there was a reply of the Sacred Congregation of the Council pertinent to the question of the place for the conferring of confirmation. The Sacred Congregation was asked:

1. May a bishop administer confirmation in a parochial church of exempt regulars against the will of these regulars?

2. Granted that in such a case a bishop may administer confirmation, may he proceed by means of invoking censures against these regulars when they impede or hinder his administration of the sacrament?

The answer to both these questions was in the affirmative.[49]

This reply of the Sacred Congregation was reaffirmed in the following century by Pope Benedict XIV.[50]

---

[45] Pars I, canon 33—Hardouin, IV, 1318.

[46] Cap. VIII: ". . . Quod si cum periculose aegrotat, se chrismatis sacramento confirmatum non esse meminerit, ac propterea id sibi ministrari petat; tunc episcopus si eo loco est, ubi ille aegrotat, ut ne sine hoc sacramento decedat, eum caritate paterna invisat et rite confirmet. . . ."—Mansi, XXXIV A, 363; cf. also, Council of Urbino (1862), Pars I, tit. V, canon 20—*Coll. Lac.*, VI, 13.

[47] *Fontes*, n. 4565.

[48] Pars Prima, *De Confirmandis:* "Hoc sacramentum potest conferri minus solemniter quocumque die, hora et loco, et causa ad arbitrium Episcopi."

[49] S.C.C., *Brixien*, 9 iul. 1657—*Fontes*, n. 2750.

[50] Const., *Firmandis*, 6 nov. 1744, § 6—*Fontes*, n. 349.

PART II

Canonical Commentary

CHAPTER VI

Existence and Gravity of the Obligation to Receive Confirmation

ARTICLE 1. AS CONSIDERED APART FROM MODIFYING FACTORS

Canon 787.—*Quanquam hoc sacramentum non est de necessitate medii ad salutem, nemini tamen licet, oblata occasione, illud negligere; imo parochi curent ut fideles ad illud opportuno tempore accedant.*

An impression that may be received from a reading of this canon is that the wording of it is ambiguous.[1] The canon states that confirmation is not necessary as an indispensable means to salvation, but it does not exclude the possibility of a necessity by reason of divine or ecclesiastical precept. Moreover, the reception of the sacrament is urged in a negative manner, and not imposed with definiteness and directness as are the paschal precept and the obligation of annual confession.[2]

Doronzo states that no direct obligation is stated in this canon, but only an indirect one of avoiding the sin of negligence in regard to this sacrament.[3] Wernz-Vidal deny that a universal and absolute precept can be proved to be imposed by this canon.[4] Nevertheless it is generally admitted that the obligation to receive confirmation does exist, and is to be found in the wording of canon 787.[5] This

---

[1] Cf. Noldin-Schmitt, III, n. 93.

[2] Cf. canon 859, § 1; canon 906.

[3] *De Baptismo et Confirmatione* (Milwaukee: Bruce, 1947), p. 368 (henceforth referred to with the name of the author).

[4] *Ius Canonicum* (7 vols. in 8, Romae: Apud Aedes Universitatis Gregorianae, 1923-1938), IV, Pars I, n. 57 (hereafter referred to with the names of the authors). See also Pistoni, *De Confirmatione a Ministro Extraordinario* (Città del Vaticano: Libreria Editrice Vaticana, 1947), n. 43 (hereafter referred to with the name of the author).

[5] Cf. canon 18; Noldin-Schmitt, III, n. 93; Genicot-Salsmans, *Institutiones Theologiae Moralis* (10. ed., 2 vols., Bruxellis: Dewit, 1922), II, n. 164 (henceforth to be referred to with the names of the authors); Ferreres,

certainly appears to be true, for the command not to neglect the sacrament could be fulfilled in no other way than by receiving it, unless a just cause for omitting the reception would be present each time an opportunity to receive were afforded.[6] The obligation of not neglecting the reception of the sacrament surely presupposes as its basis an obligation that exists by reason of the sacrament itself.

How then account for the ambiguous wording and negative character of the law? Why not a clearly defined statement of the necessity of this sacrament and of the nature of the obligation consequent upon this necessity?

The answer seems to be that the framers of this canon did not wish to be explicit.[7] They evidently had in mind the divergent theological and canonical opinion as to the gravity of the obligation to receive confirmation, and were unwilling to settle the dispute by a definitive answer.[8] Instead they indicated by the canon two extreme positions to be regarded as inadmissible; the first, that confirmation was necessary as an indispensable means to salvation; the second, that this sacrament could be neglected altogether. Between these extremes was matter of much controversy, upon which eminent authorities held opposing views. This matter the formulators of the law apparently decided to leave untouched.[9]

Compendium Theologiae Moralis ad Normam Codicis Iuris Canonici (14. ed., 2 vols., Romae: Eugenius Surbirana, 1928), II, 358 (henceforth to be referred to with the name of the author); Sabetti-Barrett, *Compendium Theologiae Moralis* (30. ed., New York, Cincinnati: Pustet, 1924), n. 675 (henceforth to be referred to with the names of the authors); Regatillo, I, n. 86.

[6] Cf. St. Thomas, *Summa Theologica,* Suppl. q. 6, a. 5; Doronzo, p. 126.

[7] Cf. Noldin-Schmitt, III, n. 93.

[8] A basis for this assertion is had in the fact that, although canon 787 is taken almost literally from the Instruction of the Sacred Congregation for the Propagation of the Faith, dated May 4, 1774, the words of the Instruction which seem to suppose a grave obligation are not included in the canon. The Instruction reads, ". . . etsi enim hoc Sacramentum non sit de necessitate medii ad salutem, tamen *sine gravis peccati reatu* respui non potest ac negligi cum illud suscipiendi opportuna adest occasio."—*Fontes,* n. 4565. Cf. Ferreres, II, n. 359.

[9] Cf. Doronzo, pp. 368-369.

It is from this controvery that an interpretation of canon 787 will have to be derived. In order that the controversy itself may be better understood, it is in order, first of all, to provide a definition of confirmation, to describe its place in the sacramental system, and to list the effects which the sacrament produces.

Confirmation may be defined as a sacrament of the New Law whereby, through the anointing with chrism and the imposing of hands, there is conferred upon a baptized person the grace of the Holy Ghost and the strength to firmly believe and vigorously profess his faith.[10]

Confirmation logically occupies second place in the sacramental system, since it is the perfection and completion of baptism.[11] Through the reception of baptism the soul is granted a spiritual rebirth and remission of sins. In confirmation the Holy Ghost is conferred upon the soul simply and fully with all His gifts to their full effusion and richness. The soul is thereby given spiritual strength so as to be at all times and in all circumstances ready to profess his faith. This sacrament, therefore, makes the recipient a soldier for the faith of Christ.[12] Among the effects produced in

---

[10] Cf. Tanquerey, *Synopsis,* III, n. 552; Cappello, *Tractatus Canonico-Moralis de Sacramentis* (5 vols., Vol. I, 5. ed., Taurinorum Augustae: Marietti, 1945), I, n. 188 (hereafter referred to with the name of the author).

[11] Conc. Trident., sess. VII, *de Sacramentis Confirmationis,* Canon 1—Denzinger, *Enchiridion,* n. 871.

[12] St. Thomas, *Summa Theologica,* pars III, q. 72, a. 5 et 7; *Summa contra Gentiles,* lib. IV, c. 60; Merkelbach, *Summa Theologiae Moralis ad Mentem D. Thomae et ad Normam Iuris Novi* (3. ed., 3 vols., Parisiis: Typis Desclée, De Brouwer et Soc., 1939), III, n. 184 (to be referred to henceforth with the name of the author).

St. Thomas illustrates the nature of confirmation and its relation to baptism by means of a comparison between the natural life and the life of the soul. "The sacraments of the New Law are ordained unto special effects of grace: and therefore where there is a special effect of grace, there we find a special sacrament ordained for that purpose. But since sensible and material things bear a likeness to things spiritual and intelligible, from what occurs in the life of the body, that which is special to the spiritual life can be perceived. Now it is evident that in the life of the body a certain spiritual perfection consists in man's attaining to the age of physical per-the recipient of confirmation is an increase of sanctifying grace and of the virtues and gifts of the Holy Ghost.[13] Among the virtues and gifts, faith and fortitude are especially augmented.[14]

The second effect of confirmation is sacramental grace, or the right to special actual graces, whereby the faith received in baptism can be uncompromisingly defended against temptations both internal and external.[15]

The third effect of confirmation is the character, or seal, by which the recipient becomes and is designated forever as a soldier of Christ.[16] This character is a spiritual power for the performance of those actions which pertain to the spiritual conflict against

---

fection and being able to perform the mature actions of a man: hence the Apostle says (I Cor., XIII: 2): 'When I became a man, I put away the things of a child.' And thence it is that besides the movement of generation whereby man receives the life of the body, there is a movement of growth whereby man is brought to maturity. So, therefore, does man receive spiritual life in baptism which is a spiritual regeneration; whereas in confirmation man arrives at perfect age or adulthood, as it were, of the spiritual life."—*Summa Theologica,* Pars III, q. 72, a. 1. (Cf. Translation by Fathers of English Dominican Province [3rd number, London: Burns, Oates & Washburn, 1923], 1, 207, from which the foregoing quotation is taken.)

[13] Council of Florence: "Effectus autem huius sacramenti est, quia in eo datur Spiritus Sanctus ad robur, sicut datus est Apostolis in die Pentecostes, annexamque habet abundantiam virtutum et septem donorum Spiritus Sancti de quibus Isaias (cap. 11, v. 2-3): 'Et requiescet super eum Spiritus Domini, spiritus sapientiae et intellectus, spiritus consilii et fortitudinis; spiritus scientiae et pietatis; et replebit eum spiritus timoris Domini.' "—Denzinger, *Enchiridion,* n. 697.

Cf. also Noldin-Schmitt, III, n. 85; Dens, p. 237.

[14] Dens, *loc. cit.*

[15] Noldin-Schmitt, III, n. 85. It is a disputed point whether sacramental grace consists only in the right to actual graces, or whether it provides, in addition, a permanent and intrinsic principle which is the basis of the title to actual graces, and itself consists in a special strength for obtaining the proper end of the sacrament. Following the latter opinion, Merkelbach (III, n. 36) describes the sacramental grace of confirmation as a "*gratia roborativa*" which increases the life of faith and brings it to maturity, at the same time giving special help against fear and human respect. See also Tanquerey, *Synopsis,* III, n. 382.

[16] Cf. Tanquerey, *Synopsis,* III, nn. 569-571.

enemies of the faith.[17] By confirmation, therefore, the faithful are dedicated to the apostolate and to Catholic Action.[18]

In view of the nature, importance and effects of confirmation, and in consequence of the temptations to the faith which every Christian is liable to encounter, it is obvious that this sacrament is a great gift of God and a boon to mankind in reaching his eternal goal.[19] Is it necessary for salvation? The Code indicates that this sacrament is not necessary as an indispensable means to salvation, which all theologians have admitted.[20] This is readily demonstrated by the fact that confirmation is a sacrament of the living and therefore presupposes the state of grace already existing in the subject.[21] But is the reception of confirmation necessary by a necessity other than that of an indispensable means? Many theologians hold that confirmation is strictly necessary by reason either of divine or, at least, ecclesiastical precept.[22] According to the doctrine of St. Thomas, all the sacraments are in some manner necessary for salvation; some are necessary in the sense that salvation cannot be obtained without them, while others are necessary for the perfection of salvation. Confirmation, accordingly, would be among those in the latter category.[23] Doronzo says that

---

[17] Cf. St. Thomas, *Summa Theologica*, pars III, q. 72, a. 5: "Character est quaedam spiritualis potestas ad aliquas actiones sacras ordinata. Iamvero per sacramentum confirmationis datur homini spiritualis potestas ad quasdam actiones sacras praeter eas quae in baptismo dantur. Nam in baptismo accipit homo potestatem ad ea agenda quae ad propriam salutem pertinent prout secundum seipsum vivit; sed in confirmatione accipit potestatem ad agendum ea quae pertinent ad pugnam spiritualem contra hostes fidei." For a thorough discussion of the precise nature of the sacramental character, consult Doronzo, *De Sacramentis in Genere*, pp. 290-317.

[18] Noldin-Schmitt, III, n. 85. For a detailed exposition of this assertion, see the work of Laras, *Confirmation in the Modern World* (Translated by George Sayer, New York: Sheed and Ward, 1938), pp. 63-112 (to be referred to henceforth by the author's name).

[19] D'Ales, *Baptême et Confirmation* (Paris: Librarie Bloud & Gay, 1928), p. 169.

[20] Cf. Doronzo, p. 364.

[21] Noldin-Schmitt, III, n. 93; Doronzo, p. 365.

[22] Cf. Ferreres, II, n. 358.

[23] *Summa Theologica*, Pars III, q. 72, a. 1, ad. 3; Coronata, I, 173.

confirmation is morally necessary for salvation in the sense that without it salvation cannot with readiness be attained.[24]

These opinions set the pattern for the controversy on the nature of the obligation to receive confirmation. Those who maintain a strict necessity insist also that a grave obligation is present. The authors who adhere to anything less than a strict necessity are unwilling to admit that a serious obligation is present.

It is this "most debated question" that the Code leaves unsettled: whether or not, apart from all aggravating or extenuating circumstances, the obligation to receive confirmation is a grave one.[25] Eminent authorities, ancient and modern, have applied their theological and canonical skill to a solution of this question without effecting anything like unanimity of opinion.[26] However, an examination of their respective arguments should provide a better understanding of canon 787, and indicate the position that must be taken in solving practical problems coming under the law.

One of the arguments advanced in favor of a grave obligation to receive confirmation is based, first of all, upon the relation of confirmation to the Christian life, and secondly, upon the fact of the institution of this sacrament by our Lord.[27] The argument is this: Just as one born corporally should arrive at maturity, so every Christian should struggle to reach spiritual perfection and, in order that he may be sure of accomplishing his purpose, should take advantage of the powers provided by Christ to avoid dangers and overcome adversaries. But such powers are those inherent in the sacrament of confirmation.[28] Moreover, when Christ instituted this sacrament as a complement of baptism in order that all men might attain the fullness of the spiritual life, He at the same time made known His will that all were obliged to receive the sacrament, provided they had the opportunity. And this obligation, since it is concerned with grave matter, must likewise be grave.

---

[24] *Op. cit.*, pp. 370-371.

[25] "Agitatissima quaestio est utrum exsistat gravis obligatio suscipiendi Confirmationem."—Coronata, I, n. 173.

[26] Cf. Cappello, I, n. 207.

[27] Cf. Sainte-Beuve, pp. 331-335.

[28] Sainte-Beuve, *loc. cit.*

Furthermore, it is of divine law, since the precept to receive it is implicitly contained in the institution of the sacrament.[29]

A second argument declares the obligation to be grave by reason of ecclesiastical precept. This argument is based principally upon two ecclesiastical documents. The first of these is the Constitution *Etsi Pastoralis* of Pope Benedict XIV (1740-1758).[30] It is stated by those who advance this argument that in this Constitution the Pope at the same time affirms the existence of an obligation and labels this obligation as grave.[31] For, after asserting universally and absolutely that Confirmation is not so necessary that one cannot be saved without it, the Pope adds that subjects ought to be warned by the ordinaries of places that those persons are to be regarded as guilty of grave sin who, though able to receive confirmation, nevertheless refuse or neglect to do so.[32] The second of these documents is a decree of the Sacred Congregation for the Propagation of the Faith, dated May 4, 1774, and having the approbation and endorsement of Pope Clement XIV (1769-1774).[33] This decree states that although confirmation is not necessary as an indispensable means to salvation, it cannot without guilt of grave sin be put off or neglected when an occasion of receiving the sacrament is available.[34]

The arguments advanced in favor of the more lenient view con-

---

[29] Cf. Aertnys-Damen, II, n. 92; Sabetti-Barrett, n. 675; Sainte-Beuve, pp. 331-335; Dens, pp. 238-240; Gury, *Compendium Theologiae Moralis* (Editio in Germania quinta, Ratisbonae: 1874), n. 270 (hereafter referred to with the name of the author); Marc-Gestermann-Raus, II, n. 1501.

[30] *Fontes,* n. 328.

[31] Aertnys-Damen, II, n. 92.

[32] Benedictus XIV, const. *Etsi Pastoralis,* 26 maii 1742: ". . . cum sacramentum confirmationis eiusmodi necessitatem non habeat ut sine eo salvus quis esse non possit; monendi tamen sunt ab Ordinariis Locorum, eos gravis peccati reatu teneri, si cum possunt ad confirmationem accedere, illam renuunt ac negligunt."—*Fontes,* n. 328.

[33] *Fontes,* n. 4565; Aertnys-Damen, II, n. 92.

[34] S.C. de Prop. Fide, instr., 4 maii 1774: ". . . etsi enim hoc Sacramentum non sit de necessitate medii ad salutem, tamen sine gravis peccati reatu respui non potest ac negligi, cum illud suscipiendi opportuna adest occasio." —*Fontes,* n. 4565; Aertnys-Damen (II, n. 92) make the point that these two decrees do not *found* the law but *teach* what is of divine law. Cf. Gury, *loc. cit.;* Marc-Gestermann-Raus, *loc. cit.*

sist, for the most part, in a refutation of the arguments just listed. The proponents of this opinion deny that the premises of their adversaries warrant the conclusion that there exists a grave obligation to receive confirmation.[35] The negative position may be outlined briefly through the claim that a serious obligation to receive the sacrament does not arise from the factors inherent in the sacrament,[36] nor from the divine law, nor from the ecclesiastical law.[37] It is reasoned that a serious obligation in this matter cannot arise from the very nature and character of the sacrament, for, if that were true, then the obligation would arise through the fact that the sacrament is necessary as an indispensable means, which supposition is universally rejected.

If it be asserted that by the natural law a person is bound to fortify himself against temptations against the faith, it may be answered that, since there are other means instituted to this end, the existence of a grave obligation to choose confirmation as a means is not conclusively established.[38] It is further argued that the crux of the question is this: when a person fails to receive confirmation on account of neglect, does God punish such neglect by withholding necessary graces? An affirmative answer to this would be contrary to the common opinion of theologians as well as to the teaching of the Roman Catechism.[39]

---

[35] Noldin-Schmitt, III, n. 93; Genicot-Salsmans, II, 164; Coronata, I, 173; Blat, *Commentarium Textus Codicis Iuris Canonici* (5 vols. in 6, Romae: Ex Typographia Pontificis in Instituto Pii IX, 1919-1927), III, Pars I, n. 82 (hereafter to be referred to with the name of the author); Lehmkuhl, *Theologia Moralis* (9. ed., 2 vols., Friburgi Brisgoviae: Herder, 1898), II, nn. 101-104 (hereafter to be referred to with the name of the author); Pruemmer, *Manuale Theologiae Moralis secundum Principia S. Thomae Aquinatis* (2. and 3. ed., 3 vols., Friburgi Brisgoviae: Herder, 1923), III, n. 161 (hereafter to be referred to with the name of the author).

[36] "Ex natura rei." Cf. Noldin-Schmitt, *loc. cit.*

[37] Cf. Noldin-Schmitt, *loc. cit.;* Genicot-Salsmans, *loc. cit.;* Pruemmer, *loc. cit.*

[38] Noldin-Schmitt (*loc. cit.*), Genicot-Salsmans (*loc. cit.*). However, Aertnys-Damen (III, n. 92) attack the validity of this rebuttal, for they argue that the effect proper to confirmation is not obtained without at least the desire for the sacrament, and what is obtained by the desire of the sacrament does not release one from the obligation of an actual reception.

[39] Noldin-Schmitt, *loc. cit.; Catechism of the Council of Trent,* p. 182.

Against the opinion which places the source of obligation in the divine law, it is denied that the very fact of the institution of the sacrament by our Lord gives rise to a strict obligation to take advantage of its benefits, for this would assume that Christ could not institute means helpful to salvation without making them gravely obligatory.[40] To the argument that God wishes all to attain the perfection of the spiritual life, which is an effect proper to confirmation, the proponents of the less strict view reply that God indeed desired all the faithful to attain essential perfection or the state of grace, but that it remains a point to be proved that He wanted all to attain the accidental perfection conferred through confirmation.[41]

The point that is given most prominence by both sides is the argument drawn from ecclesiastical authority. Much attention is paid to the Constitution *Etsi Pastoralis* and to the previously mentioned Instruction of the Sacred Congregation for the Propagation of the Faith, for they offer the clearest statements with reference to the question in the whole controversy. These statements appealed to many theologians as compelling arguments in favor of the existence of a grave obligation to receive Confirmation.[42] Yet their opponents were not without weighty reasons for rejecting these documents as substantiating the opposite claim. The argument from Pope Benedict's Constitution, *Etsi Pastoralis,* is rejected on the grounds that the document concerns only a particular case, together with all the circumstances peculiar to it, and therefore cannot be the source of a universal law.[43]

The particular situation about which the Pope's letter was concerned involved a group of Italo-Greeks who were refusing the

---

[40] Cf. Doronzo, p. 366.

[41] Noldin-Schmitt, *loc. cit.;* Genicot-Salsmans, *loc. cit.*

[42] Aertnys-Damen, *loc. cit.;* Marc-Gestermann-Raus, *loc. cit.;* Pruemmer (III, 161) says that St. Alphonsus, at first holding the milder view, believed that there was no precept, natural or positive, which could be adduced as favoring the existence of a grave obligation, and that it was only later, when he felt that Pope Benedict XIV stated the contrary opinion, that he deserted the more lenient view on account of Benedict's authority.

[43] Coronata, I, 173.

reception of confirmation, because the use of the Eastern custom of confirmation after baptism had been denied to them. Accordingly those who deny a strict obligation maintain that, when the Pope taught that these people would be guilty of mortal sin in refusing confirmation, he was referring to a mortal sin of contumacy, and not affirming a serious obligation, in general, to receive the sacrament.[44]

The alleged force of the document of the Sacred Congregation for the Propagation of the Faith was accorded a similar refutation in its nature of an argument for the existence of a serious obligation to receive confirmation. In the first place, so it is argued, the Congregations are not competent to solve questions of morals, or to settle controversies among theologians.[45] Furthermore, this document, inasmuch as it was an Instruction sent to priests empowered by papal indult to administer confirmation, was in consequence of a particular character, and not such as to institute universal law.[46] Finally, even if such a document had formulated a universal law, it is asserted that the words of the Instruction, "*tamen sine gravis peccati reatu respui non potest ac negligi,*" can be understood as pointing exclusively to a contempt of the sacrament. That the presence of a contempt for any of the sacraments constitutes a mortal sin is something which is of course universally admitted.[47]

In view of the opposing stands taken by eminent and respected authorities, sympathy can be had for the view of Ferreres (1861-1936), namely, that the obligation is in greater probability a grave

---

[44] Cf. Woywod, *A Practical Commentary on the Code of Canon Law* (10. ed., 2 vols., New York: Wagner, 1946), I, n. 688 (hereafter referred to with the name of the author).

[45] Coronata, I, 173.

[46] Cf. Woywod, *loc. cit.*

[47] Cf. Coronata, I, 173. Marc-Gestermann-Raus (II, n. 1501), who defend the opinion which maintains the existence of a serious obligation, accuse their adversaries of inverting the correct meaning of these texts, and Gury (n. 270) disagrees with the interpretation which limits the text of the Constitution *Etsi pastoralis* to the particular situation among the Italo-Greeks. Cappello (I, 207), however, who likewise favors the stricter opinion, admits that these texts are not the basis of valid arguments for the stricter opinion.

one, though such an obligation cannot with certainty be demonstrated.[48]

Fortunately there is a practical stand to be taken precisely because of such disagreement. Aertnys-Damen, who are among the most ardent supporters of the existence of a strict obligation, concede that in practice their position cannot be urged in the face of the strong opposite doctrine on the part of weighty authors.[49] In view of the fact that so many great minds have pondered the question and yet have not concluded to the presence of a grave obligation, it must be conceded that extrinsic authority is had for the milder opinion, and that the law cannot be urged as one of serious obligation.[50]

Having established the existence of an obligation to receive confirmation, and having determined that for practical purposes this obligation in itself, as apart from all modifying factors, is a light one, one then comes to the point of examining how prospective recipients are affected by this obligation. It is to be remarked first of all that, since the obligation exists, it logically follows that all who are subjects for the valid and lawful reception of this sacrament are bound by the obligation unless they are legitimately impeded from receiving the sacrament.[51] Even those who, because of their age or condition, cannot of themselves fulfill the obligation, are nevertheless fundamentally bound to receive this sacrament provided that they can receive it validly and lawfully. Under such circumstances the fulfilling of the obligation must be cared for primarily by the parents or such other persons who stand

---

[48] "Haec obligatio probabilius gravis sit, sed certo non constet." *Op. cit.*, II, n. 358. Cf. Jone, *Moral Theology* (Englished and adapted to the Code and Customs of the United States of America by Rev. Urban Adelman, Westminster: Newman Bookshop, 1945), n. 488 (henceforth referred to with the name of the author).

[49] *Op. cit.*, II, 93.

[50] Cf. Davis, *Moral and Pastoral Theology* (4. ed., 4 vols., London: Sheed and Ward, 1945), I, 95-96 (hereafter referred to with the name of the author).

[51] Cf. canon 786; Cappello, I, 202.

in their stead.[52] Between each subject for the valid and lawful reception of confirmation and the sacrament itself there stands the relationship of an obligation. In the following pages each class of recipients will be considered, and an effort will be made to determine how each class is affected by its duty to receive this sacrament, and to what extent this duty will sometimes be incumbent upon others than the recipients themselves.

In the consideration of each class of recipients it will be assumed that confirmation has certainly not been previously received. When a prudent doubt exists as to the previous reception or the validity of the same, the sacrament should be repeated conditionally.[53] Such a procedure is required when the subject is about to receive first tonsure or to enter a religious novitiate.[54] He should also then be persuaded of this step when marriage is being contemplated.[55] However, the doubt must be a truly sufficient one, that is, it must have inherent in it a greater degree of probability than is required of the doubt which suffices to justify a conditional rebaptism.[56] For, when it is truly probable that Confirmation has been received, not even one who is about to receive Sacred Orders should be compelled to be conditionally reconfirmed.[57]

The first class of recipients is that of adults who are free from

---

[52] S.C. de Prop. Fide, instr., 4 maii 1774: "Ceterum missionarii non omittant populos sibi creditos etiam hortari ut Confirmationem debito tempore recipiant, nec non ut parentes filios suos confirmari curent. . . ."—*Fontes,* n. 4565.

S. C. de Sacramentis, decr., 8 aug. 1910: "Obligatio praecepti confessionis et communionis quae puerum gravat, in eos praecipue recidit qui ipsius curam habere debent, hoc est in parentes, in confessarium, in institutores et in parochum. . . ."—*Fontes,* n. 2103. Although this decree refers to the reception of confession and communion, the same principle would be involved in the reception of confirmation.

[53] Canon 732, § 2: "Si vero prudens dubium exsistat num revera vel num valide collata fuerint [sacramenta], sub conditione iterum conferantur." Cf. Regatillo, I, n. 86.

[54] Canon 974, § 1, n. 1; canon 544; cf. Regatillo, *loc. cit.,* S.C.S. Off., instr. 2 apr. 1879—*Fontes,* n. 1060.

[55] Canon 1021, § 2; Regatillo, *loc. cit.*

[56] Cf. Marc-Gestermann-Raus, II, 1499.

[57] Cf. Marc-Gestermann-Raus, *loc. cit.*

parental authority.[58] This class of recipients evinces the least complex factors for the evident reason that the individual stands alone in the obligational relationship to the sacrament of confirmation. It is his primary duty to see that the obligation is discharged, for it is only through a devolved obligation that anyone else must aid him in fulfilling this duty.[59] Outside the danger of death the individual in this case is held to discharge his obligation when the bishop is present and prepared to administer the sacrament, and the baptized person has no legitimate reason for deferring the reception of the sacrament.[60] Not to present himself for the reception of the sacrament would under these circumstances entail the guilt of negligence.

The circumstance of death is something which makes general obligations become specific and more urgent. For example, there is the general obligation to pray. One of the occasions when this obligation becomes specific is the hour of death, should the dying person be without the state of grace.[61] In like manner there is a special obligation to receive Holy Communion when the danger of death is present.[62] Accordingly the obligation to receive confirmation seems to take on additional binding force for a person when he is in danger of death, for then there presumably is offered the final opportunity for the fulfillment of the law. However, according to the doctrine of St. Thomas, the obligation would not be gravely binding even then, even though a person's non-reception of the sacrament implies his forfeiture of greater glory in heaven.[63] The subject's charity toward himself would therefore seem to make an additional demand that he avail himself of this last opportunity to receive a blessing that is beyond comparison

---

[58] Cf. canon 88, § 3. The term "adult," as used throughout this thesis, will signify one who, either prior to or after being seven years of age, has reached the use of reason and thus has become responsible for his acts.

[59] This devolved obligation would first of all fall upon the parents or those who hold their place in relation to the recipient. It would attach to the recipient's baptismal sponsors in the event of a default on the part of the parents or of those who hold their place.

[60] Cf. Sainte-Beuve, p. 335; Dens, p. 240.

[61] Cf. Davis, II, 7.

[62] Cf. Davis, III, 227-229.

[63] *Summa Theologica,* pars III, q. 73, a. 8, ad. 4.

with earthly riches, and by reason of which he will appear in the Resurrection, not as an imperfect Christian, but as one marked as a soldier of Christ.[64]

It is in danger of death that the words of canon 787, *"oblata occasione,"* are of particular application. For since it is the common opinion that a bishop at least probably has no obligation to administer confirmation to the dying, it seems to follow that an opportunity for receiving the sacrament would not at all times be available to such persons.[65]

Although the bishop is held to provide the sacrament to those who legitimately and reasonably request it, he is generally regarded as not being bound for the reason simply that the request comes from someone who is in danger of death.[66] It is argued that if the bishop were to administer the sacrament in one instance and deny it in another, scandal would be likely to result; and yet if he attempted to make himself available for every such case, he would impose upon himself a very heavy burden.[67] The majority opinion has additional support when the reception of confirmation is sought by one who is afflicted with a contagious disease.[68]

Coleman offers compelling arguments to justify a departure from the common opinion.[69] His arguments are drawn from what distinguished theologians, such as St. Thomas and Suarez, had to say on the administration of confirmation in danger of death, from a consideration of certain particular legislation having the Holy See's approval, and from the solicitude of the Holy See itself to

---

[64] St. Thomas, *loc. cit.;* Blat, III, Pars I, n. 82.

[65] Cf. Coleman, *The Minister of Confirmation,* The Catholic University of America Canon Law Studies, No. 125 (Washington, D. C.: The Catholic University of America Press, 1941), pp. 87-94 (to be referred to hereafter with the name of the author).

[66] Canon 785, § 1. "Episcopus obligatione tenetur sacramentum hoc subditis rite et rationabiliter petentibus conferendi, praesertim tempore visitationis dioecesis."

[67] Cf. Lehmkuhl, II, 137; Noldin-Schmitt, III, 90; Coleman, p. 88.

[68] Coronata (*op. cit.,* I, 169), while not subscribing to the majority opinion, concedes its application in a case wherein the danger of contracting a contagious disease is present. Cappello (*op. cit.,* I, 200) is reluctant to yield even on this point.

[69] *Op. cit.,* pp. 88-94.

have confirmation made available for those who are in danger of death.[70] Cappello, maintaining the same view, holds that a bishop is obliged to give confirmation to the dying, provided that he can conveniently do so.[71]

Fortunately the decree *Spiritus Sancti munera* of the Sacred Congregation of the Sacraments, of September 14, 1946, provides a twofold solution to this problem.[72] In the first place the wording of the decree seems to favor the view that is held by the minority, for it appears to presume an obligation on the part of the bishop to respond to requests for confirmation when they are received from dying persons. For this decree, in conferring to pastors and certain other priests the faculty to confirm those who are in danger of death, warns the recipients of the faculty that they may exercise it, "provided that the diocesan bishop is *unavailable* or is *lawfully prevented* from conferring confirmation in person, and that there is at hand no other bishop in communion with the Apostolic See, even though only a titular bishop, who could without serious inconvenience take the other's place."[73] Zerba describes this passage as "safeguarding the right of bishops."[74] However, whatever may have been the primary intention of the Sacred Congregation in including the section just described, the wording as used seems to indicate that an obligation on the part of the bishop is presumed.

A second and far more important service rendered by this decree is one which all but obviates the problem of the bishop's disputed absence of obligation to confirm the dying. That service is found in the very purpose of the decree which was to make the sacra-

---

[70] *Loc. cit.*

[71] *Op. cit.*, I, n. 200.

[72] *AAS*, XXXVIII (1946), 349.

[73] ". . . dummodo Episcopus dioecesanus haberi non possit vel legitime impediatur quominus Confirmationem per se ipse valeat conferre, nec alius praesto sit Episcopus communionem habens cum Apostolica Sede, licet titularis tantum, qui sine gravi incommodo ipsi suffici queat."

Cf. Hannan, *The Jurist* (Washington, D. C., 1941-), VII (1947), 211-233.

[74] *Commentarius in Decretum* "SPIRITUS SANCTI MUNERA" (Città del Vaticano: Libreria Editrice Vaticana, 1947), n. 19. (Henceforth the author's name will be used in the citing of this work.)

ment of confirmation more available to the dying by providing additional ministers of the sacrament.[75] Moreover, there hardly can be any question of the obligation of these ministers to use the faculty for the purpose for which it was expressly provided.[76] The only exception to this statement is had in the case of an epidemic that is dangerous to life, when according to the common opinion a pastor is required to administer only the necessary sacraments.[77]

The adult, when still subject to parental authority, does not stand alone in relation to the obligation to receive confirmation. For in addition to his own obligation there is a duty incumbent upon his parents, which duty is based upon justice, to see that the child's obligation is discharged when an opportunity for receiving the sacrament is afforded.[78] Moreover, some authors hold this obligation on the part of parents to be a grave one. Cappello states that the virtue of piety makes this duty gravely incumbent on the part of parents.[79] A similar opinion on the part of Ferreres is more noteworthy, since he is of the school that holds that there is only a light obligation to receive confirmation.[80] However it is difficult to see how a grave obligation is binding upon parents, while only a light one is incumbent upon the children.

Infants are subjects for the valid reception of confirmation.[81] Radically or fundamentally they are subject to the obligation to receive confirmation. But this obligation is to be discharged through

---

[75] Cf. Pistoni, nn. 89-92.

[76] Cf. canon 785, § 2. "Eadem obligatione tenetur presbyter privilegio apostolico donatus, erga illos quorum in favorem est concessa facultas." Canon 467, § 1. "Debet parochus officia divina celebrare, administrare sacramenta fidelibus quoties legitime petant. . . ." Canon 468, § 1. "Sedula cura et effusa caritate debet parochus aegrotos in sua paroecia, maxime vero morti proximos, adiuvare, eos sollicite sacramentis reficiendo eorumque animas Deo commendando."

Cf. Hannan, *ibid.*, p. 231; Zerba, nn. 34-35.

[77] Cf. Coleman, p. 96; Lehmkuhl, II, 51.

[78] Cappello, I, n. 207; Davis, II, 73.

[79] Cappello, I, 207.

[80] "Obligatio tum parentum, tum parochorum, curandi ut filii vel subditi suscipiant hoc sacramentum gravis esse videtur." Ferreres, II, 359.

[81] Cf. canon 786; Cappello, I, 202; Coronata, I, 172. Cf. also canon 88, § 3. The term "infant" will be used throughout this treatise in the sense of one who has not yet acquired the use of reason.

the medium of their parents or of those who are responsible for them.[82] Outside the danger of death, however, and unless there are just and grave reasons justifying the minister to decide otherwise, the fulfillment of this duty is to be deferred until the subject has arrived at approximately the age of seven, in order that the sacrament may be received with greater profit.[83] Should there be present just and grave causes by reason of which the minister will decide to dispense with the age requirement, the obligation to receive the sacrament would automatically be in force, and the infant's parents by yielding to the judgment of the minister would be bound to co-operate in the discharge of the infant's obligation.[84]

In danger of death the barrier of age is withdrawn, and infants not only may receive confirmation, but ought to receive it. Parents should be taught that they have a responsibility to take steps lest the child depart from this life deprived of a great blessing which is his due as a Christian.[85]

Equivalent to infants in the eyes of the law are the habitually demented.[86] They can receive confirmation validly and lawfully and since, by reason of their incapacity to think normally, an obligation cannot be imposed directly upon them, it is incumbent upon someone else to make provision for their reception of the sacrament.[87] It is true that they may never be exposed to the spiritual combat, but their affliction is only an accidental condition, and inasmuch as they are fundamentally capable of becoming soldiers of Christ, they are not to be denied the benefits of the sacrament through no fault of their own.[88]

---

[82] Cf. canon 12. Since the law which imposes the reception of confirmation as an obligation is not a purely ecclesiastical law, infants and those who are equivalent to infants are not exempt by reason of the rule which is stated in canon 12.

[83] Canon 788.

[84] Cf. Resp. S.C. de Sacramentis, 30 iun 1932—*AAS,* XXIV (1932), 271; Bouscaren, I, 348-349; Cappello, I, 203; Coronata, I, 174. The just and grave causes contemplated in the canon shall be considered in a later chapter dealing with the age of the recipient.

[85] Cf. St. Thomas, *Summa Theologica,* pars III, q. 72, a. 8, ad. 4; Blat, III, pars I, n. 82.

[86] Canon 88, § 3.

[87] Cf. Merkelbach, III, n. 190; Marc-Gestermann-Raus, II, n. 1499.

[88] Cf. Aertnys-Damen, II, n. 90.

Obviously provision for the conferral of confirmation must be made through the medium of the parents or the guardians. The problem is easily solved when the insane persons are placed in institutions that are regularly visited by the bishop at the time of his diocesan visitation.[89] Should the subject be confined to a place that is not included in the bishop's visitation, then it is within the scope of the parents' obligation to arrange, through their pastor, for a private conferral of the sacrament. This should be done at a time when the bishop is reasonably near, and can conveniently fulfill their request. It seems likewise to be a part of their obligation to make such arrangements as are necessary with the authorities of the institution to insure a courteous reception of the bishop, and a dignified conferral of the sacrament.

Institutions for the insane are generally in the hands of civil authorities. When friendly relations can be established with these authorities, the institutions should be a regular object of the bishop's visitation. When an attempt to gain admittance to such places, even for a private conferral of the sacrament, would only bring odium upon the Church, then it seems better to omit the conferral of the sacrament than to militate against the common good.[90] However, this does not mean that parents and others who are responsible for the spiritual welfare of the inmates of these institutions should adopt a weak and compromising attitude in this regard, especially when so great a good as the blessing of confirmation is at stake. Unless it is evident that the Church would suffer harm thereby, they should insist upon their rights as citizens not to have the exercise of their religion unreasonably restricted.[91]

Pastors and others who by reason of the recent decree *Spiritus Sancti munera* enjoy the faculty of confirming persons who are in danger of death should visit such institutions as exist in their parishes and find out whether any of the Catholic patients are not

---

[89] Cf. canon 786, § 1.

[90] Cf. Coleman, p. 95.

[91] It is evident from canons 787 and 788 that the reception of confirmation is an integral part of the Catholic religion.

confirmed.[92] Should he be called upon to administer the last sacraments to such patients, he would then be able to confer confirmation also, provided that the bishop is not available.[93] Therefore the pastor should inform physicians, nurses and attendants attached to hospitals and other institutions, of his extraordinary power to confer confirmation, in order that his faculties may be made available to patients in danger of death.[94]

With regard to the habitually demented who have never had the use of their mind, those who are responsible for them should see to the discharge of their obligation at the earliest possible time. If an opportunity occurs while the subject is still an infant, it should be taken advantage of, since there is no point in waiting for a chance of recovery that is only remote, in the hope that a more fruitful reception may be realized. It could readily happen that such an opportunity would never occur again. Should the subject be in danger of death, then no effort should be spared that the dying person's soul may become enriched with the blessings of confirmation.[95]

---

[92] *AAS,* XXXVIII (1946), 349.

The faculty to confirm within the limitations stated in the decree was given to the following and to them exclusively:

a) Pastors entrusted with their own territory to the exclusion of personal or family pastors, unless they are entrusted with their own territory, even though cumulatively with other pastors;

b) Vicars mentioned in canon 471 and vicars econome;

c) Priests to whom is exclusively and unconditionally (*stabiliter*) entrusted the complete care of souls with all the rights and obligations of pastors in a definite territory and with a definite church.

Cf. Hannan, "Decree on the Administration of Confirmation to Those in Danger of Death through Illness," *The Jurist,* VII (1947), 211-233; Bastnagel, "Parochial Vicars and the Faculty to Confer Confirmation," *The Jurist,* VII (1947), 174-179; Zerba, nn. 20-25; Pistoni, nn. 93-99.

[93] Cf. *Spiritus Sancti munera—AAS,* XXXVIII (1946), 349.

On October 25, 1948, the provisions of this decree were extended to chaplains permanently attached (*"stabiliter addicto"*) to maternity hospitals. In the event that there were several chaplains in one hospital, only the chief chaplain would enjoy this faculty. The faculty could be exercised only in the event that the bishop of the diocese, or even some other bishop in communion with Rome, or the pastor of the place were unavailable or legitimately impeded from conferring the sacrament. Cf. *The Jurist,* IX (1949), 261-262.

[94] Cf. Pistoni, nn. 89-91.

[95] Cf. Pistoni, *loc. cit.*

Concerning the habitually demented who intermittently have the use of their mind, the presence or absence of the danger of death will be a factor in deciding whether their obligation urges at a particular time, or whether the reception is to be deferred until a more propitious moment. Outside the danger of death the period when the subject enjoys the use of his mind is a more favorable time for the reception of confirmation. The recipient can then be instructed as to the nature and dignity of the sacrament, and can prayerfully dispose himself for a more fruitful reception.[96] Therefore, when there is no reason to believe that death is imminent, the subject who lacks the use of his mind should not receive the sacrament until at a more favorable time when he will enjoy the use of his faculties. A deferral in this case would be gravely necessary should the patient have lapsed into insanity when evidently not in the state of grace.[97]

The presence of the danger of death would modify the picture to some degree. It would be fortunate if the subject were in possession of his mind, so that he might not only discharge his obligation, but at the same time dispose himself for a more fruitful reception. However, although the use of reason is not being enjoyed, the danger of death will rule out any postponement. The sacrament is to be given even though the recipient has not requested it, for his will to receive it can be presumed from the fact of his being a Catholic.[98] Likewise the state of grace is to be taken for granted unless the contrary is clearly evident.[99]

ARTICLE 2. AS CONSIDERED IN RELATION TO MODIFYING FACTORS

It was seen in the previous article that, because of a divided opinion on the question and because of the absence of a seriously obliging law in the Code, the obligation to receive confirmation, apart from all modfying factors, is for practical purposes not to be regarded as gravely binding. Nevertheless, it is likely that there

---

[96] Cf. Coronata, I, 172.

[97] Cf. Regatillo, I, n. 85; Suarez, *De Sacramento Confirmationis,* q. 72, art. 8, sec. 2, n. 4—*Opera Omnia,* XX, 670.

[98] Cf. Regatillo, *loc. cit.;* Suarez, *loc. cit.*

[99] Cf. Regatillo, *loc. cit.;* Suarez, *loc. cit.*

will in many cases be present objective circumstances and subjective considerations which will be such as to intensify, to diminish, or even to eliminate completely the obligation of receiving the sacrament of confirmation.

In the following pages the different classes of recipients will be considered, together with the various factors that may modify their obligation to receive confirmation.

With reference to adults who are not in danger of death and who at the same time are free from parental authority, the factor of a considerable distance to be traveled for the reception of the sacrament would eliminate, at least for the time being, the obligation to receive it. For, obviously, if the sacrament is being administered at a place too far distant to be taken advantage of, it could not be said that an opportunity for its reception was afforded.[100] Not the question of physical impossibility, but that of moral impossibility, or of serious inconvenience, is being considered here. What distance to be traversed would constitute a hardship serious enough to justify the foregoing or the postponing of the reception of the sacrament would depend on other factors, e.g., the person's physical constitution or his financial means. A greater distance would be required in the case of a normally healthy person as contrasted with one who is infirm. The same would be true of a person financially well-off as compared with one who would be considered inconvenienced by paying for his transportation to the place of the conferral of the sacrament. Moreover, since normally the obligation cannot be urged as being grave, a lesser distance than that which would be required for an excuse from the fulfillment of the paschal precept would be sufficient, since the latter law is certainly gravely binding.[101]

Another external circumstance that merits consideration is the question of scandal. If because of particular circumstances the omission of confirmation on the part of someone would give rise to scandal, there would be a proportionately graver obligation to receive the sacrament.[102]

---

[100] Canon 787.

[101] Canon 859, § 1.

[102] Cf. Dens, p. 238; Coronata, I, 173; Doronzo (p. 371), holding the opinion that only by reason of contempt would the non-reception of confirmation

The shame or embarrassment that an adult might experience at being confirmed with a group of children could be a factor that would diminish his obligation to receive.[103] This difficulty is greatly obviated in some of the larger cities of this country where confirmation ceremonies for adults are held several times a year. However, where this practice is not in vogue, it is recommended that the subject be firmly encouraged to receive the sacrament. This act of encouragement should however be given in such a manner that the existence of the obligation will be neither imprudently belittled nor unduly magnified.[104]

If a nurtured contempt stood as an obstacle to the reception of confirmation, then indirectly the called for obviation of this contempt could give rise to a grave obligation to receive the sacrament.[105] In this case the obligation itself to receive confirmation would remain a light one, but there would be a grave obligation to remove the existing obstacle. Once the obstacle was duly eliminated, the sacrament would naturally be received. There are some authors who maintain that contempt can hardly be absent when a person does not make use of his opportunity to receive Confirmation.[106] According to St. Thomas, however, contempt is not necessarily present when someone omits the reception of a sacrament which is not necessary for salvation.[107] Contempt would certainly be present, however, if someone were to look upon the sacrament

---

be seriously sinful, admits that incidentally the occasioned scandal consequent upon the non-reception of the sacrament could be a factor equivalent to that of contempt, so that the law would impose a serious obligation for the reception of the sacrament.

[103] Cf. Cappello, I, 207; Noldin-Schmitt, III, 93; Regatillo, I, 86.

[104] Cf. Cappello, I, 207; Noldin-Schmitt, III, 93; Regatillo, I, 86.

[105] Cf. St. Thomas, *Summa Theologica,* Pars III, q. 65, art. 4, ad. 3: "Omnium sacramentorum contemptus est saluti contrarius." See also Doronzo, pp. 370-371, who maintains that according to St. Thomas the only instance in which the non-reception of confirmation would be seriously sinful is the case where the act of omission is motivated through contempt.

[106] Cappello, I, 207; Coronata, I, 173.

[107] *Summa Theologica,* Pars III, q. 65, art. 4, ad. 3; "Non tamen est contemptus sacramenti, ex hoc quod aliquis non curat accipere sacramentum quod non est de necessitate salutis."

as something of trifling importance, or as something vile or childish, or as only a meaningless ceremony.[108]

Inasmuch as one of the particular effects of confirmation is the moral strength which it confers for the overcoming of temptations against the faith, it is clear that some, either because of their own mental constitution, or because of the peculiar temptations to which they are exposed, have greater need of this sacrament than do others. Therefore a person who is particularly predisposed to disbelief, or who is strongly inclined to doubt or skepticism, would be gravely bound to receive confirmation.[109] The same would hold true of the faithful in general in times of persecution, or in the case of anyone who is exposed to the loss of his faith, as can happen in places where bad example, perverse books and secularistic papers greatly endanger faith and piety.[110]

Such conditions can be said to prevail in our own country, where our people are constantly exposed to pagan and irreligious influences.[111] Therefore it can be upheld as an almost universal rule that the faithful of this country are seriously bound to receive confirmation when the opportunity is provided them. This view seems to be substantiated by the concern on the part of the Fathers of the Plenary Councils of Baltimore that all the faithful be fortified through the reception of confirmation against the danger of the loss of their faith. [112]

---

[108] Cf. Dens, p. 238.

[109] Cf. Coronata, I, 173.

[110] Cf. Sainte-Beuve, p. 333; Dens, p. 240.

[111] "Equidem qui inter haereticos versantur, plurimis fidei negandae periculis obnoxii, vix possunt absque gravi culpa negligere subsidium quo infirmitas eorum roboretur."—Kenrick, *Theologia Moralis* (3 vols., Mechliniae, 1861), II, n. 11 (henceforth to be referred to with the name of the author).

[112] "Licet vero hoc sacramentum non sit necessarium de necessitate medii ad salutem, nihilominus est necessarium de necessitate praecepti iis omnibus, qui jubentis Dei et Ecclesiae praecepta intelligere et adimplere possunt. Quod praecipue valet de iis, qui persecutionem pro religione patiuntur, aut gravioribus contra fidem tentationibus mortisve periculo exponuntur. Quo enim gravius periculum, eo major se munendi necessitas."—*Concilii Plenarii Baltimorensis II Acta et Decreta,* n. 250.

". . . Unusquisque igitur Episcopus saltem unoquoque triennio totam dioecesim perlustrare teneatur, non solum . . . , sed etiam ut fideles tot amittendae fidei in hac regione periculis expositos Sacramento Confirmationis munire possit. . . ." *Concilii Plenarii Baltimorensis III Acta et Decreta,* n. 14. Cf. Coleman, pp. 86-87.

The approach of death seems all the more strongly to demand early effort to dispel an attitude of contempt which has caused anyone to omit the sacrament. Likewise, in danger of death the one who particularly needs strength against temptations contrary to faith is all the more urgently under obligation to receive the sacrament when the final opportunity to do so is at hand.

What has been said of the factors which augment or diminish the obligation to receive confirmation as applied to adults free from parental authority, applies as well to those adults who are subject to their parents. The chief difference is that in this class of recipients the responsibility to see that the obligation is fulfilled devolves ordinarily upon the parents, and accordingly it is with reference to them that modifying circumstances could determine a greater or lesser degree in the obligation of the reception of the sacrament. Thus, for example, an occasion of scandal could arise out of the fact that one who was known to be a Catholic impeded his child in the reception of confirmation.[113] Such a situation can be visualized as happening in this country where confirmation classes are regularly held in the parochial school in anticipation of the bishop's visitation. If under these circumstances any Catholic parent without sufficient reason withdrew his child from confirmation instructions, or interfered in any way with the child's reception of the sacrament, his action would not only be detrimental to the child's welfare but in addition would occasion grave scandal. In this matter the existing obligation of the parent toward the child would be proportionately augmented.[114]

Outside the danger of death the obligation of infants would ordinarily not be affected by modifying factors, since the fulfillment of their obligation normally awaits the time when they are beyond the stage of infancy.[115] However, in danger of death, or for reasons which are to be considered later, the normal age for the reception of confirmation would have to be anticipated, and it can readily be seen that many of the factors that would affect the obligation in the cases that have already been contemplated with reference to

---

[113] Cf. Dens, pp. 238-239.

[114] Cf. Cappello, I, 207.

[115] Cf. canon 788.

other classes of recipients would likewise be of application in the cases of parents or of guardians with reference to the infants under their care. Factors of this kind could be such as those of contempt or of scandal, which of their nature are not restricted to any particular category of recipients.

Such factors as are not limited to any one group can also be conceived as applying to the habitually demented who sometimes experience lucid intervals, and to the parents and guardians of those habitually insane who have never known the use of reason. But in addition to these there are other modifying circumstances that apply only to those who are responsible for the spiritual welfare of persons afflicted with insanity.

For example, the physical condition of the patient may be such as to make the conferral of confirmation morally impossible, or to become the occasion for considerable disrespect in the act of the sacrament's administration. There would, then, be no obligation to have confirmation administered if the patient were in such an advanced stage of his affliction that the reception of the sacrament would most likely be attended with an act of violence and irreverence. However, such dangers would have to be truly present, and should not, when they do not really exist, be conjured up as a pretext for shirking responsibilities.

Again, the attending physician may reasonably judge that the conferral of confirmation upon his patient at that particular time would cause undue excitement, which would retard the patient's chances of recovery. In such a case the reception of the sacrament could be deferred until a more opportune time.

In the case of the habitually demented one could visualize an instance paralleling that of an adult of advanced age who is reluctant to receive confirmation among a group of children.[110] Similarly, sympathy can be had for parents who are ashamed to have their mentally retarded offspring, even though not confined to a mental hospital, receive the sacrament along with normal children of his age. Moreover, there could readily take place an unseemly spectacle that would be detrimental to the dignity of the sacrament. In addition, the inclusion in a confirmation group of a child

---

[110] Cappello, I, 207.

which is incapable of absorbing Christian doctrine[117] could cause untoward wonderment, if not also an irrepressible resentment, among the children who had arduously prepared themselves for the coming of the bishop.

However, although these considerations would lessen the parents' obligation, they would not remove it altogether, for in view of the feasibility of a private conferral under the circumstances of the bishop's presence in the parish, when he senses his obligation to confirm those who legitimately and reasonably request the sacrament,[118] it can rightly be said that an opportunity to receive the sacrament is present.[119]

Finally, entrance into the higher callings of the religious life and the clerical state makes imperative the reception of confirmation by which one becomes a perfect Christian.[120] Also the vocation of Matrimony, in consideration of the lofty purposes of that state, calls for the previous reception of confirmation when a considerable hardship would not be thereby imposed.[121] It does not appear, however, that this requirement points to a grave obligation.[122]

Scholion. The duty of pastors to urge the due and opportune reception of confirmation.

One of the means employed by the Church to have the faithful comply with their obligation to be confirmed is that of the pastoral instruction. Realizing that the people can love and desire only what they know, the Church requires as a pastoral duty that the children be prepared at stated times each year for the reception of confirmation by means of instructions extending over a number of days.[123]

It is obvious that the questionable degree of gravity in the obligation to receive confirmation should not constitute the subject

---

[117] Canon 786.

[118] Cf. canon 785, § 1.

[119] Cf. canon 787.

[120] Canon 544, § 1; canon 974, § 1, n. 1.

[121] Canon 1021, § 2.

[122] Cf. Regatillo, I, 86.

[123] Cf. canon 1330, 1°; Woywod, II, n. 1350; Coronata, *Institutiones Iuris Canonici* (2. ed., 5 vols., Taurini: Marietti, 1939-1947), II, 917.

matter of a sermon or instruction.[124] Even though the pastor is convinced that the obligation is grave, he should not run the risk of forming erroneous consciences by expressing his views on the matter. And to teach the milder opinion would be likely to minimize the sacrament's importance in the eyes of the faithful. Moreover, the seriousness or lightness of the obligation to receive confirmation is not the criterion of the sacrament's value. Its importance is, instead, to be measured by the marvelous effects of grace which it produces. And if these are presented to the people in a manner suited to their understanding, a great deal will have been done to eliminate negligence, and to promote an increased appreciation for the sacrament, which is especially needed now on account of the paganizing influences of the present times.[125]

These instructions will be all the more effective if they are accompanied with a pastoral solicitude which makes certain that none of the flock are remiss in their obligation to receive the sacrament. The pastor, mindful of the value of confirmation, will keep a special watch over those who may be weak in the faith, and by advice and encouragement will seek to bring about a fruitful reception of the sacrament for them as well as for those who are under their care.[126] Finally, he will always be ready to make available to the dying the use of the faculties which have been shared with him as an extraordinary minister of the sacrament.[127]

---

[124] Regatillo, I, 86: "Cum de gravi obligatione suscipiendi hoc sacramentum non constet, non est de ea sermo faciendus."

[125] Cf. Blat, III, Pars I, 82; Jone, n. 488.

[126] Cf. Blat, *loc. cit.*

[127] Cf. decr. *Spiritus Sancti munera*—*AAS,* XXXVIII (1946), 349.

CHAPTER VII

The Age for the Reception of Confirmation

Canon 788—*Licet sacramenti confirmationis administratio convenienter in Ecclesia Latina differatur ad septimum circiter aetatis annum, nihilominus etiam antea conferri potest, si infans in periculo mortis sit constitutus vel ministro id expedire ob iustas et graves causas videatur.*

ARTICLE 1. THE LAW IN RELATION TO ORDINARY CIRCUMSTANCES

Before coming to a consideration of the specific age suited for the reception of confirmation as enunciated in the law, one should treat of a preliminary question which is based upon the position that confirmation occupies in the sacramental system, since a solution of this problem is of import in the determining of the most appropriate age for the receiving of this sacrament. This introductory question is concerned with the order of temporal succession between confirmation and first Holy Communion, and although at the time when confirmation in the Latin Church ceased to be administered immediately after the conferral of baptism there existed some variations in practice, it has consistently been the mind of the Church that confirmation should precede the reception of first Holy Communion.[1]

That the mind of the Church calls for the conferral of confirmation before the reception of first Holy Communion is clear from the documents emanating from the Holy See. These expressly state what is the correct order of temporal succession. In one of

---

[1] Cf. Cappello, I, 203; Lehmkuhl, II, 102; Wernz-Vidal, IV, Pars I, n. 56; "Confirmation before First Communion," *The Ecclesiastical Review* (originally *The American Ecclesiastical Review*, Philadelphia, 1889-1943; Washington, 1944), XCVIII (1938), 160-164. The author of this article asserts that where practices contrary to the mind of the Church took place, they can be explained on the basis of necessity, and as cases wherein the practices dictated by expediency came to be looked upon as meeting with the Church's approval.

the Church's official instructions is found the declaration that previously confirmation should be administered, and later on, in due time, first Holy Communion should be provided.[2] This viewpoint of the Holy See was again expressed in a statement of Pope Leo XIII, who said that before children are refreshed with the heavenly banquet of the Eucharist they should first be sealed with the sweet oil of the sacrament of confirmation, and thereby they would experience richer graces from their reception of Holy Communion.[3] As recently as 1932 it was officially stated that it was more appropriate and more in conformity with the nature and effects of confirmation, if children be restrained from approaching the Holy Table for the first time, until after they have received this sacrament.[4]

A scrutiny of these documents of the Holy See reveals that implicitly contained in them are traditional concepts of the Church, especially those which have to do with the subordination of confirmation and of all the other sacraments to the Eucharist. In the first place the Church has never ceased to look upon confirmation as the complement of baptism.[5] St. Thomas, when speaking of the order of the sacraments, stated that baptism, which is a spiritual regeneration, clearly occupies first place; confirmation is next in order, since it is intended for the formal perfecting of power; and after these comes the Eucharist, through the reception of which is intended the achievement of final perfection.[6]

---

[2] Resp. S.C.C., 10 mart. 1854: ". . . prius locus sit confirmationi, postea vero, opportuno tempore, primae Communioni suppeditandae." *Collectaneo S.C. de Prop. Fide*, I, n. 1105.

[3] Ep., *Abrogata*, 22 iun. 1897: ". . . visum tibi est in mores dioecesis tuae inducere ut pueri, antequam divino Eucharistiae epulo reficiantur, christianum confirmationis sacramentum, almo inuncti chrismate suscipiant. . . . Porro sic confirmati adolescentuli ad capienda praecepta molliores fiunt, suscipiendaeque postmodum Eucharistiae aptiores, atque ex suscepta uberiora capiunt emolumenta."—*Fontes*, n. 634.

[4] S. C. de Sacramentis, Resp. 30 iun. 1932: ". . . opportunum esse et conformius naturae et effectibus sacramenti Confirmationis, pueros ad sacram Mensam prima vice non accedere nisi post receptum Confirmationis sacramentum." Bouscaren, I, 349.

[5] Cf. Galtier, "L'Age de la Confirmation," *NRT*, LX (1933), 675-686.

[6] "Manifestum est quod Baptismus, qui est spiritualis regeneratio, est prius; et deinde Confirmatio quae ordinatur ad formalem perfectionem virtutis; et postmodum Eucharistia, quae ordinatur ad consecutionem finis."—*Summa Theologica*, pars III, q. 65, a. 2.

It is also the teaching of St. Thomas that all the sacraments are directed to the Eucharist as to an end or purpose. For the sacrament of Orders serves for the consecration of the Eucharist, the sacrament of matrimony for its symbolization, and the other sacraments serve at least for a more worthy reception of the Holy Eucharist.[7]

How, precisely, does confirmation dispose the child for a more fruitful reception of his first Holy Communion? First of all, through confirmation the soul acquires a spiritual maturity, and thus becomes better able to understand and appreciate the sacrament of the Eucharist.[8] Moreover, the virtues and gifts of the Holy Ghost act as repellents to fear, shame and human respect, which might deter the subject from approaching the Holy Table.[9]

Since it is clearly the mind of the Church that confirmation should precede the reception of first Holy Communion, it follows that any episcopal or conciliar legislation would be invalid if it denied the reception of confirmation to those who had not yet made their first Holy Communion.[10] On the other hand, the Church has made it clear that it does not wish to exclude from the reception of Communion those children who have reached the age of discretion, but who have not yet been able to receive confirmation.[11]

---

[7] *Summa Theologica,* pars III, q. 65, a. 3; cf. Council of Trent, sess. 13, can. 3—Denzinger, *Enchiridion,* n. 846; Merkelbach, III, n. 101.

[8] Leo XIII, ep. *Abrogata,* 22 iun. 1897—". . . ad capienda praecepta molliores fiunt."—*Fontes,* n. 634.

[9] St. Thomas, *Summa Theologica,* pars III, q. 65, a. 3, ad 4; Farrell, *A Companion to the Summa* (4 vols., New York: Sheed and Ward, 1939-1942), IV, 267; Vermeersch, *Theologia Moralis Principia Responsa Consilia* (3. ed. auctior et emendatior, 3 vols., Romae: Università Gregoriana, 1945-1947), III, n. 246 (henceforth to be referred to with the name of the author).

[10] Cf. Leo XIII, ep., *Abrogata,* 22 iun. 1897—*Fontes,* n. 634; Cappello, I, 203; Coronata, I, n. 174.

[11] Resp. S. C. de Sacramentis, 30 iun. 1932: ". . . non tamen iidem censendi sunt prohiberi quominus ad eandem mensam prius admittantur, si ad annos discretionis pervenerint, quamvis Confirmationis sacramentum antea accipere non potuerunt."—*AAS,* XXIV (1932), 271; Bouscaren, I, 349; Regatillo, I, n. 87: Coronata, I, n. 174; "Instruction on the Age for Confirmation," *ER,* LXXXVII (1932), 513-515.

For the obligation annually to receive Holy Communion seriously binds one who has reached the age of reason.[12] It is debatable, however, that a like degree of moral compulsion attends the reception of confirmation.[13]

It can readily be seen that the ideally preferable procedure of having confirmation precede first Holy Communion will have to yield in many instances to physical or moral impossibility. In view of the large territory and population of some dioceses, as compared with only one or several bishops to administer the sacrament, it is obvious that the ideal will not always be attainable. Very often the faithful would suffer serious spiritual detriment, if the reception of their first Holy Communion had to wait an opportunity to receive confirmation. Accordingly the practically adaptable procedure is to have confirmation precede the reception of first Holy Communion in the episcopal city and in the other cities and districts in so far as that is possible, but in other cities and districts where this arrangement cannot prevail, to have the conferral of confirmation be as near as is feasible to the day of first Holy Communion.[14]

Although confirmation may be validly received at any age,[15] the period of a person's life which the Church deems most opportune for the reception of the sacrament in order that the recipient may best profit by its graces is about the age of seven. Even though up to the thirteenth century confirmation was administered immediately after the conferral of baptism, the Church believes a

---

[12] Canon 839, § 1.

[13] Cf. Cappello, I, n. 203; Coronata, 1, n. 173; Aertnys-Damen, II, n. 92.

[14] § 1 . . . in Civitate archiepiscopali pueri ad primam Communionem admitti non debent ante sed solum post susceptionem Confirmationis, utputa postridie.

§ 2 Extra vero Civitatem archiepiscopalem, si annus aut periodus visitationis pastoralis cum anno seu periodo primae Communionis coincidat, pueri pariter ad primam Communionem non admittantur ante sed post susceptionem Confirmationis; secus, ad primam Communionem utique admitti poterunt cum ad annos discretionis pervenerint, ad normam canonis 854, quamvis confirmationis sacramentum antea recipere non potuerint." *Acta et Decreta Synodi Dioecesanae Quebecensis II* (1940), decr. 192. Cf. Cappello, I, 204.

[15] Cf. Dens, p. 284; Aertnys-Damen, II, n. 89.

more fruitful reception is to be had by deferring the sacrament's administration until the subject's acquired age of discretion.[16]

It has been suggested that the reason in the early Church for the practice of confirming infants was the following. During the centuries when persecution was rampant, it was believed that children would have need of the graces of confirmation immediately upon reaching the age of discretion, at which time a battle for the Faith would almost surely have to be undergone.[17] However, it seems more reasonable to suppose that the concept of confirmation as the complement of baptism dictated the practice of bestowing both sacraments on the same occasion, but that later on, with the spread of the Church and the impossibility of the bishop's presence at the time of each subject's baptism, the advantages of a later conferral came to be realized.[18]

One of the benefits to be derived from the deferring of the reception of the sacrament until the age of reason is first of all the opportunity to provide some instruction, calculated to result in a knowledge and appreciation of the nature and meaning of confirmation, and in a consequent better reception.[19] Moreover, the danger of irreverence connected with the confirming of infants is eliminated when the subject is an adult. Likewise the possibility of a repeated administration of the sacrament is more adequately excluded inasmuch as an adult will in all normal instances remember that he has already received the sacrament, and thus will not present himself for a repeated reception of it.[20]

If a wholehearted conformity with the law of the Church is to result, then there should be no appreciable delay in the reception

---

[16] Canon 788; Coronata, I, n. 174; Aertnys-Damen, *loc. cit.*

[17] Dens, *loc. cit.*

[18] Cf. "Confirmation before Holy Communion," *ER,* XCVIII (1938), 160-164; Galtier, "L'Age de la Confirmation," *NRT,* LX (1933), 675-686.

[19] Resp. S. C. de Sacramentis, 30 iun. 1932—*AAS,* XXIV (1932), 271; Bouscaren, I, 349; Dens, p. 234; Marc-Gestermann-Raus, II, n. 1499; Merkelbach, III, n. 192; Kenrick, *Baptism; Also a Treatise on Confirmation* (Baltimore: 1852), p. 233; Noldin-Schmitt, III, n. 91; Vermeersch, III, n. 246.

[20] Dens, *loc. cit.;* Marc-Gestermann-Raus, *loc. cit.;* Merkelbach, *loc. cit.;* Vermeersch, *loc. cit.*

of confirmation after the age of reason has been reached.[21] It is with the dawn of reason that the struggle against temptation begins, and it is an injustice to deprive children for a number of years of that sacrament which is so adequate a weapon in the bitter struggle against the wickedness of the devil and against the illusions of the world and the flesh.[22] Moreover, the beginning of the age of reason is the ideal time for the reception of confirmation not only because instruction adequate for a profitable reception can be imparted, but also because at that age children are not far enough removed from their baptismal innocence to have become tainted with perverse influences.[23]

The fact that the Church has made provision in the law for anticipating the age of reason under certain circumstances, but has not made any provision for delaying beyond that stage, is an indication that the Church is strongly disposed toward early confirmation.[24] Of similar import is the fact that highly regarded canonists consider the probable danger, namely that children will otherwise be without the advantages of confirmation for some time after the age of discretion, a sufficient warrant for the conferring of the sacrament in advance of the usual time.[25]

Since the law states that the administration of confirmation is to be deferred until about the seventh year, the law is adequately

---

[21] ". . . non tamen diutius est differenda, sed convenienter datur ad septimum circiter aetatis annum."—Merkelbach, III, n. 192. "Rationis usu adepto, expedit Confirmationem non diu differre, sed praevenire aetatem passionum, priusquam pueri graviter peccare incipiant."—Aertnys-Damen, II, n. 90.
. . . , differatur ad septimum aetatis annum quando usum rationis (puer) habere praesumitur, non ultra illam aetatem ex Ecclesiae approbatione." Blat, III, pars I, n. 83.

[22] Decr., *Spiritus Sancti Munera—AAS*, XXXVIII (1946), 349; Aertnys-Damen, *loc. cit.*

[23] Cf. Laymann, *Theologia Moralis* (2 vols., Patavii, 1733), II, lib. V, tract. III, cap. V, p. 258 (hereafter to be referred to with the name of the author).

[24] Canon 788; S. C. de Sacramentis, instr. 20 maii 1934—Bouscaren, II, 185-188.

[25] Cf. Blat, III, pars I, n. 83; Creusen, "*L'Age de la Confirmation dans L'Eglise Latine, NRT,* LVIII (1931), 825-826; Jone, n. 488.

observed if normally children received the sacrament when six, seven or eight years of age.[26] The question then suggests itself, is there an allowable delay after the recipient's acquired use of reason? It appears that a considerable delay is not permissible.[27]

Since the bishops of the United States are required to complete the visitation of their entire dioceses within a period of three years,[28] there appears to be no reason why the recipients of confirmation should not, as a rule, be within the age-span of from six to nine years. Where such a law *"Praeter Codicem"* is not in effect, bishops are called upon by the Code to complete the visitation of their dioceses within a period of five years.[29] Under this arrangement none of the children about to receive should normally be beyond the age of ten or eleven. As shall be seen presently, the situation of such a belated reception can be circumvented by means of an anticipation of the normal age of reception whenever it can be foreseen that by the time of the next episcopal visitation these subjects would be considerably more than seven years of age.[30] Moreover, since under these conditions it is licit for a bishop to confirm children under the age of discretion, it is apparently obligatory for him to do so, for otherwise these subjects would suffer the spiritual detriment of being without confirmation for a period of time during which they are legally entitled to it.[31]

Despite the evident mind of the Church as to the suited age for the reception of confirmation, there are some who favor a later administration of the sacrament at ages ranging from ten to four-

---

[26] Cf. canon 18. This observation is made in view of the wording of the canon itself, apart from any consideration with respect to the time of first Holy Communion.

[27] Cf. Merkelbach, *loc. cit.;* Aertnys-Damen, *loc. cit.;* Blat, *loc. cit.;* Woywod, I, n. 689.

[28] *Concilii Plenarii Baltimorensis III Acta et Decreta,* n. 14. This decree has not been abolished by the appearance of the Code. Cf. canon 22; Barrett, *A Comparative Study of the Councils of Baltimore and the Code of Canon Law,* The Catholic University of America Canon Law Studies, n. 83 (Washington, D. C.: The Catholic University of America, 1932), p. 67.

[29] Cf. canon 343, § 1; canon 785, § 1; Ferreres, II, n. 355.

[30] Cf. canon 788; S. C. de Sacramentis, instr. 20 maii 1934—Bouscaren, II, 185-188.

[31] Cf. Coleman, p. 95.

teen. Some prefer a deferral of the sacrament until this age in order that the subject may in his approach to confirmation be fortified with a more thorough knowledge of Christian doctrine.[32]

Others believe that a conferral at the beginning of adolescence is more in keeping with the idea of confirmation, in as much as they regard this sacrament as consummating and perfecting the mystery of man's spiritual regeneration.[33] Moreover it is thought that one who is to become a soldier of Christ should undergo due preparation for that event by means of appropriate exercises designed to give him the courage befitting one who accepts this dignity.[34] Consequently it is felt that the significance of confirmation can be best brought home to the children by pointing their religious instruction to the reception of confirmation as the coronation of their religious formation, and as an event marking their formal enrollment in the Christian army.[35]

Still others advocate a more advanced age for confirmation as a measure of expediency in order to keep children in attendance at religious instruction. It is attested to by experience that some persons regard the reception of confirmation as the termination of their children's need for religious instruction, and once this sacrament has been received, the children are withdrawn from the Catholic schools and from catechism classes.[36]

With regard to the requisite degree of instruction in Christian

---

[32] Cf. Kinane, "A Plea for Early Confirmation," *The Irish Ecclesiastical Record* (Dublin, 1864-), V Series, XLI (1933), 307-309.

[33] Cf. Galtier, "L'Age de la Confirmation," *NRT,* LX (1933), 675-686.

[34] Galtier, *ibid.,* pp. 685-686.

[35] Galtier concedes that there are advantages to having confirmation administered at the age of discretion, but believes it opportune to explore the arguments favoring conferral at a more advanced age, a plan with which he is apparently in sympathy.—"De trouver la conclusion logique, n' empêche d'ailleurs pas de reconnaitre les avantages de la pratique contraire. Seulment, il a paru legitime de signaler l'appui que peut trouver ici l'usage seculaire en nos pays de retarder la confirmation jusqu' a l'age de 10 ou 12 ans. Ceux qui l'estiment plus favorable a la formation solide de l'adolescence chretienne ne sauraïent etre que heureux de le voir ainsi compris a Rome."—*Ibid.,* p. 686.

[36] This is the reason usually given in explanation of diocesan statutes which require a minimum age of twelve or fourteen.

doctrine, it is evidently unreasonable to demand appreciably more religious knowledge in preparation for confirmation than is required for the reception of first Holy Communion, inasmuch as the reception of confirmation is supposed to precede that of first Holy Communion.[37] In the reception of first Holy Communion a full and perfect knowledge of Christian doctrine is not exacted. Only so much knowledge is required that the child can understand according to his capacity those mysteries of the faith that are absolutely necessary for his salvation, and at the same time be able to distinguish the Bread of the Eucharist from ordinary bread.[38] It is sufficient that the child should afterwards learn the entire catechism gradually and according to his ability.[39]

Since confirmation is to precede first Communion, the same amount of knowledge should be adequate, except that the child's knowledge of confirmation should be proportionate to the knowledge he is expected to have of the Eucharist in order to make his first Communion worthily.[40] Moreover, the proposal to postpone confirmation until the time of adolescence, in order to make this sacrament the culmination of the religious training, seems in principle to be affected with the error which Pope Leo XIII criticised in his epistle *Abrogata.*[41] For this suggestion would out of due proportion emphasize the importance of confirmation in the light of this sacrament's subordination to the Eucharist.

While every effort to give confirmation the recognition and prominence it deserves should be encouraged, it is another matter to stress this sacrament in such a way as to detract from the reverence which is owed to the Blessed Eucharist. For it must be remembered that, while all the other sacraments contain the power of Christ, the Holy Eucharist contains Christ Himself.[42] There-

---

[37] Cf. Pistoni, n. 23; Kinane, *loc. cit.*

[38] Cf. Canon 854, § 3; S. C. de Sacramentis, decr. *Quam singularis,* 8 aug. 1910—*Fontes,* n. 2103.

[39] Kinane, *loc. cit.*

[40] Cf. Kinane, *loc. cit.;* Pistoni, *loc. cit.*

[41] 22 iun. 1897—*Fontes,* n. 634.

[42] Conc. Trident., sess. XIII, cap. 3: ". . . verum illud in ea excellens et singulare reperitur, quod reliqua sacramenta tunc primum sanctificandi vim habent, cum quis illis utitur; at in Eucharistia ipse sanctitatis auctor ante usum est."—Denzinger, *Enchiridion,* n. 876.

fore confirmation should be received at a time that proves most advantageous to the subject in the light of his reception of the Eucharist, which time is that which coincides with the dawn of reason.

Finally, it is to be admitted that the importance of retaining youths under religious instruction should not be underestimated. However, to endeavor to secure this end by requiring a more advanced age for the reception of confirmation than the age specified by the Church is a measure which cannot be justified even on the basis of expediency.

In the first place, if particular law would demand an age of ten, twelve or fourteen years for the reception of confirmation, which would imply an added period of from three to seven years beyond the time at which according to the mind of the Church the sacrament is most opportunely conferred, then the subjects eligible for confirmation would for that added period of time be deprived of its needed graces.[43] In view of the nature and the effects of confirmation, an early conferral of this sacrament seems to be especially needed by those who are awaiting the opportunity to discontinue their course of religious instruction. Their apparent unwillingness to submit to anything more than the minimum of religious training appears to indicate a family background of laxity and indifference. In such a situation it seems that the supernatural aids of confirmation would prove more timely and beneficial than would a prolonging of their course in the catechism. Moreover, to delay the conferral of the sacrament to others with a view to benefiting this particular class of recipients would impose an injustice upon those children whose parents have no intention whatever of removing them from the classes of Christian doctrine.

In addition, when confirmation is postponed for an appreciable time after the age of reason, it is to be presumed that in the natural course of events some of those who are eligible for the reception of the sacrament will die without having received it.[44] Even in view

---

[43] Cf. canon 788; Kinane, *loc. cit.*

[44] Cf. decr. *Spiritus Sancti munera*—*AAS*, XXXVIII (1946), 349; Hannan, "Decree on the Administration of Confirmation to Those in Danger of Death through Illness," *The Jurist*, VII (1947), 221.

of the pastor's faculty to confirm those who are in danger of death through illness, it is quite possible that some children will die unconfirmed because the pastor was not able to reach them in sufficient time to confer the sacrament. It is also readily conceivable that the danger of death could be present to children by reason of causes other than illness, in which cases the pastor could not validly confirm them.[45] Hence, it is apparently unfair, with reference to those who are eligible recipients, deliberately to withhold confirmation beyond the time at which the Church acknowledges them to be eligible for its reception.

There seem to be several inconsistencies involved in a plan whereby religious instruction would serve for several years as a substitute for a divinely instituted means of grace. For it is a part of Christian doctrine that one of the special effects of confirmation is to provide strength for the battle against temptation which begins with the dawn of reason,[46] and therefore Church law has provided that this sacrament be conferred at about the age of seven.[47] To delay the administration of confirmation until such time has elapsed as will be necessary to provide a thorough course in Christian doctrine seems to be a self-contradictory process.

The idea of having the deferral of confirmation until the age of twelve or fourteen serve as a safeguard against the failure to receive religious instruction is evidently based on the principle that it is preferable to have a child equipped with both confirmation and adequate training in Christian doctrine, than to have him confirmed but wanting as to a thorough grounding in religious principles. Nevertheless, this plan has in its disfavor that for a period of from three to seven years—critical ones in the child's religious formation—a supernatural aid is foregone in favor of a natural one. It needs by no means to be assumed that this procedure provides the only effective remedy for the problem that calls for a solution. Wherever such a high degree of religious indifference is evidently present, what guarantee is there that some youths will not desert their Christian training anyway, perhaps never to take

---

[45] Hannan, *ibid.*, p. 228.

[46] Cf. Aertnys-Damen, II, n. 90.

[47] Canon 788.

advantage of an opportunity to be confirmed? For the problem there should be found some other solution which does not contravene the law of the Church with regard to the suited age for the reception of confirmation,[48] and which is not out of harmony with the order of temporal succession that is to be observed in the administering of the sacraments.[49]

ARTICLE 2. THE LAW IN RELATION TO EXTRAORDINARY CONTINGENCIES

The Church requires that confirmation be deferred until about the age of seven, for it is at that age that the Church believes ideal conditions will most likely surround the reception of the sacrament.[50] However, when these favorable circumstances are not going to prevail, or when the hope for their existence is counterbalanced by other grave and urgent considerations, then the reasonableness of postponing the reception of confirmation disappears, and the Church wisely makes provision in such cases for an early reception of the sacrament.[51]

There obviously cannot exist any reason for postponing the conferral of confirmation when a child is exposed to the danger of death. It is certainly preferable to receive the sacrament under circumstances that are not most favorable, than to run the risk of not receiving it at all. And it is to be noted that the threat of death need not necessarily come from illness, since the law makes no restriction to that effect. Consequently the ordinary minister of the sacrament could confirm an infant which enjoys the best of health, but which at the same time is truly exposed to the danger of death by reason of a persecution, a plague, or any other cause.[52]

---

[48] Canon 788.

[49] Cf. St. Thomas, *Summa Theologica*, pars III, q. 65, a. 2.

[50] Cf. Marc-Gestermann-Raus, II, n. 1499; Merkelbach, III, n. 192; Dens, p. 234.

[51] Cf. canon 788.

[52] It is to be observed that the powers conferred by the decree *Spiritus Sancti munera* are restricted to the cases in which there exists a real danger of death as deriving from a serious illness from which it is foreseen that the person will die. Nevertheless this limitation of the faculty is not to be understood as precluding the pastor's right to confirm anyone who in

Among the just and grave reasons that warrant an administration of the sacrament prior to the subject's age of reason, legitimate custom must be given a place.[53] There can be no question of this assertion today, inasmuch as a certain amount of speculation on this point resulted in an affirmative decision by the Sacred Congregation of the Sacraments.[54]

The word *"convenienter"* of canon 788 had led some to surmise that this law of the Code was directive only, and not preceptive. It was thought that the provisions of this law were merely of counsel, and therefore did not exert any binding force.[55] A reply of the Pontifical Commission for the Interpretation of the Code, dated June 16, 1931, corrected that erroneous impression when it gave an affirmative reply to the question whether canon 788 was to be understood in the sense that in the Latin Church the sacrament of confirmation cannot be conferred before the age of about seven years, except in the cases mentioned in the canon.[56]

This response gave rise to further speculation which had as its object the ancient customs prevailing in Spain, in Latin America and in the Philippine Islands, namely of conferring confirmation upon infants before the age of reason, or even immediately after baptism. An opinion came forth immediately that the response was aimed directly at these customs.[57] It was believed that after

---

danger of death by reason of any intrinsic affection of the human organism, even though it may have originally arisen from a wound. Cf. Hannan, *ibid.*, p. 228.

[53] Canon 5. "Vigentes in praesens contra horum statuta canonum consuetudines sive universales sive particulares . . . , quae quidem centenariae sint et immemorabiles, tolerari possunt, si Ordinarii pro locorum ac personarum adiunctis existiment eas prudenter submoveri non posse; . . . "

Canon 27. ". . . sed [consuetudo] neque iuri ecclesiastico praeiudicium affert, nisi fuerit rationabilis et legitime per annos quadraginta continuos et completos praescripta; . . ."

[54] Resp., 30 iun. 1932—Bouscaren, I, 348-349; Coronata, I, n. 174.

[55] Cf. Noldin-Schmitt, III, n. 91; Coronata, I, n. 174.

[56] *AAS*, XXIII (1931), 353; Bouscaren, I, 348. Cf. Creusen, "L'Age de la Confirmation, dans L'Eglise Latine," *NRT*, LVIII (1931), 825-826.

[57] "Igitur videtur Commissio Pontifica intendisse cum primis percutere morem, in Ecclesia Latina alicubi adhuc extantem, conferendi indiscriminatim pueris et infantibus cuiuscumque aetatis Sacramentum Confirmationis:

this reply of the Code Commission these ancient customs could no longer be sustained unless just and grave reasons were present to justify them.[58]

Accordingly a question regarding the legitimacy of this custom was proposed to the Sacred Congregation of the Sacraments.

The answer given by that Congregation was:

"In the affirmative, and according to the mind of the Church; the mind of the Church is that unless grave and just causes interfere, the administration of the sacrament of confirmation should be deferred until about the age of seven. According to canon 788, where a contrary custom prevails, the faithful should be diligently taught the law of the Latin Church respecting the administration of confirmation after proper catechetical instruction, which, as experience teaches, helps to refine the minds of youths, and strengthens them in Catholic doctrine."[59]

In the light of this response it is now generally conceded that the customs referred to therein may be included among the just and grave causes spoken of in canon 788.[60] The reply is interpreted to mean that where these ancient customs exist it is to be presumed that they are founded upon just and grave reasons, and that it is not required to demonstrate that assumption as an incon-

---

porro is casus peculiariter attingit Hispania, Americanam Latinam et Insulas Philippinas."—Maroto, "De Aetate Confirmandorum," *Apollinaris* (Romae, 1928-), IV (1931), 372-377, and in particular 375-376.

[58] Cf. canon 5; Maroto, *loc. cit.* In this article, however, Maroto cites post-Code authors, Ferreres (II, n. 357) and Aertnys-Damen (II, n. 81), as holding the view that these customs reflect the existence of just and grave causes which would constitute an exception to the general rule.

[59] S. C. de Sacramentis, 30 iun. 1932: "Affirmative et ad mentem. Mens est ut ubi sacramenti Confirmationis administratio differri potest ad septimum circiter aetatis annum, quin obstent graves et iustae causae ad normam c. 788 contrariam consuetudinem inducentes, fideles sedulo edocendi sunt de lege communi Ecclesiae Latinae, praemissa sacrae confirmationis administrationi illa catechesis instructione, quae tantum iuvat ad animos puerorum excolendos et in doctrina Catholica solidandos prout experientia docet"—*AAS*, XXI (1929), 276; Bouscaren, I, 348-349. Cf. Coronata, I, n. 174.

[60] Cf. Coronata, I, n. 174; Wernz-Vidal, IV, Pars I, n. 56; Regatillo, I, n. 87.

trovertible fact. However, when it is clear that just and grave causes for the extant custom have ceased to be present, then an attempt should be made to effect its disappearance. This should be accomplished, not by means of a decree which abolishes the custom, but through an endeavor to induce a new usage which is consonant with the common law, the continuance of which usage is then to receive support from the faithful who have become duly instructed in the universal law of the Latin Church on this point.[61] Moreover, it is maintained that the Sacred Congregation of the Sacraments wished to make clear by this decree that the existence of an admissible contrary custom in one locality was not a sufficient reason for introducing this custom elsewhere. The Congregation had the future in mind as well as the past, and wished to express itself as disapproving such customs that would form without having just and grave reasons to warrant their existence or continuance.[62]

Another cause regarded as sufficiently just and grave to warrant the conferral of confirmation at an age below the prescribed time for its reception is present when it can be prudently foreseen that the succeeding visit of the bishop, or of the priest if he be endowed with the faculty of confirming, will not take place until after a long period of time has elapsed.[63] When difficulty of travel through mountainous territory or any other similar cause conspires to prevent the bishop from visiting certain regions of his diocese except after prolonged intervals of time, the likely result is that in the natural course of events some will die without ever having received the sacrament, and others will remain unconfirmed for years beyond the prescribed age of reception, unless some provision is made to meet this contingency.[64] Consequently it is not only reasonable but also a matter of provident pastoral care, to allow for exceptions to the law, in order that the benefit of confirmation

---

[61] Cf. Maroto, "De Aetate Confirmandorum," *Commentarium pro Religiosis* (Romae, 1920- from 1935; *Commentarium pro Religiosis et Missionariis*), XII (1932), 250-254; Cappello, I, 205.

[62] Cf. Galtier, "L'Age de la Confirmation," *NRT*, LX (1933), 675-686.

[63] Cf. S. C. de Sacramentis, instr. 20 maii 1934—Bouscaren, II, 185-188; Coronata, I, n. 174.

[64] Cf. S.C.C., *Segovien*, 12 mart., 23 apr. 1774—*Fontes*, n. 3788.

may yield to those who are affected with circumstances that otherwise would preclude the gaining of that benefit.

The question suggests itself, to what extent may this principle be applied in practice? How far below the age of reason may a child be admitted to the reception of the sacrament? There is an opinion that when a bishop of an extremely large diocese, particularly one of mountainous territory, foresees that he will not be able to return to a particular locality for a period of four or five years, then he may include among his confirmants children of six, five, or four, or even those who are but three or two years of age.[65] The reason advanced for this opinion is the fact that otherwise these children would remain too long exposed to the devil's wiles, unprotected by the graces of confirmation.[66]

The following norm may be suggested for adoption. When the foreseen absence is such that the child's reception of confirmation would thereby be delayed until after the age of eight, it will be legitimate to confer the sacrament regardless of the recipient's present age. For the phrase *"septimum circiter aetatis annum"* inherently signifies the age of six, seven, or eight, and moreover the word *"antea"* which is employed in the canon does not imply any restriction as to the number of years below seven, when an exception to the general rule is warranted.[67] Since in the face of truly justifying circumstances it is lawful to confirm those who are below the age of reason, it is a merely incidental matter just how far removed from the age of reason the recipients happen to be, as long as the minister of the sacrament takes sufficient precautions to avoid all danger of possible abuse as resulting from his mode of action.

Since the foreseen absence of the bishop over a long period of time warrants an anticipation of the time for the reception of the sacrament, the same would hold true in favor of certain individuals with reference to whom in particular the bishop's absence would

---

[65] Cf. "Instructio pro Simplici Sacerdote Sacramentum Confirmationis Sedis Apostolicae Delegatione Administrante: Annotazione," *Il Monitore Ecclesiastico* (Romae, 1876-), V Series, VII (1935), 111-113; Coleman, p. 95.

[66] "Instructio pro Simplice Sacerdote . . ." *loc. cit.;* Coleman, *loc. cit.*

[67] Canon 788.

be foreseen.[68] A child whose parents are about to change their residence to some remote territory, or an offspring of those whose lot it is to travel from place to place, so that in either case it can reasonably be conjectured that, unless the permission to receive confirmation is here and now conceded, the child is not going to have a similar opportunity to receive this sacrament for some time after he acquires the use of reason, would in this respect be equivalent to those who are subject to only infrequent visits on the part of the bishop.

Other eventualities suggest themselves as exceptions to the normal procedure. Among them may be included the threat of persecution in consequence of which a child, when it is nearing the age of reason, will have need of the strength of the sacrament as soon as that stage of his life is reached.[69] Another case which could lend justification for a departure from the law is the situation in which a pastor, having for years endeavored to persuade religiously indifferent parents to have their children confirmed, finally has succeeded in obtaining their promise to do so. If among the children one or several are below the age of reason, but are likely to be exposed to parental neglect in the future, then there exists a sufficient reason to include these children also among the recipients of confirmation, provided of course that the occasion for scandal be duly obviated in the case.

It is the prerogative of the minister of the sacrament to decide in all cases whether the attendant causes are sufficiently serious to warrant an exception to the rule which calls rather for the deferring of the administration of the sacrament until the age of seven.[70] However, in interpreting the law he should guard against any over-lenient tendency which could readily lead to a custom of conferring the sacrament indiscriminately without regard to age.[71] Consequently the minister would not regard such factors as the pious wishes of the parents, or the chance opportunity of administering the sacrament to someone bound to him by ties of blood

[68] Cf. Pistoni, n. 22.

[69] Dens, p. 284.

[70] Canon 788.

[71] Resp. S. C. de Sacramentis, 30 iun. 1932—Bouscaren, I, 348-349.

or of friendship, as just and grave causes for allowing an exception to the law.[72]

An overly strict interpretation that would disregard just claims for an early reception is likewise to be avoided. The recognized likelihood that some may die without the sacrament, or that some may be required to remain unconfirmed for several years beyond the age of discretion, presents an element of emergency that warrants the anticipated conferring of the sacrament.[73] In coming to a decision as to the merit of the causes involved, the minister can profitably ponder the opinion of Cappello, who teaches that the words of canon 788, *"ob iustas et graves causas,"* are to be interpreted from a moral approach and in an elastic sense, namely, as pointing to any cause which is reasonable and truly just in the prudent judgment of the bishop.[74]

If in line with this opinion the danger of death and the foreseen absence of the bishop for a considerable period are to qualify as reasonable and truly just causes, they must possess a degree of probability which counterbalances the likelihood of a more fruitful reception at a later time when the recipient has reached the use of discretion. The benefits that accompany the reception of confirmation which takes place at the time when reason has been acquired should likewise serve as a measuring rod in the act of determining whether the attendant circumstances present sufficiently reasonable and truly just causes for not awaiting the legal age of reception. For unless the reasons for administering the sacrament here and now are proportionate to the reasons which evince the advantages that the recipient can gain by awaiting the age of reason, the decision to sanction a premature conferral of confirmation would work an injustice to the subject involved, in the sense namely that such a decision would deprive the recipient of his right to the more fruitful reception of the sacrament at a later time in his life.

---

[72] Creusen, "L'Age de la Confirmation dans L'Eglise Latine," *NRT,* LVIII (1931), 825-826.

[73] Cf. Creusen, *loc. cit.;* Blat, III, pars I, n. 83; Jone, n. 488.

[74] "Putamus *gravitatem* sumendum esse *moraliter* et *lato* sensu, ita ut quaelibet causa *rationabilis et vere iusta* ex prudenti Episcopi iudicio sufficiat." *De Sacramentis,* I, n. 202.

CHAPTER VIII

CONDITIONS REQUIRED IN THE RECIPIENT OF CONFIRMATION

Canon 786. *Aquis baptismi non ablutus confirmari nequit; praeterea, ut quis licite et fructuose confirmetur, debet esse in statu gratiae constitutus et, si usu rationis polleat, sufficienter instructus.*

ARTICLE 1. FOR THE VALID RECEPTION OF THE SACRAMENT

When the sacrament of confirmation is validly and fruitfully received both the character and the graces proper to the sacrament are obtained. If all the conditions are present for the valid reception of the sacrament, but some condition is wanting which is necessary for its fruitfulness, then the character of confirmation is indeed conferred, but the graces that are ordinarily bestowed are withheld. Should some factor that is essential for the valid reception be lacking, then neither the sacramental character nor the graces are acquired by the recipient.[1]

Fundamentally requisite for the valid reception of confirmation is the fact of a previous valid baptism of water. The character bestowed in confirmation supposes the presence in the soul of the baptismal character, for, as St. Thomas stated, the relation of baptism to confirmation is like that of birth to growth, and just as a person cannot grow to maturity unless he first be born, so also a person cannot be confirmed unless he first be baptized.[2] Consequently, if confirmation were administered to an unbaptized person, then, as St. Thomas expressly stated the case, he would receive nothing.[3]

---

[1] Cf. Coronata, I, n. 34, et n. 172.

[2] "Cuius ratio est quia ita se habet confirmatio ad baptismum, sicut augmentum ad generationem. . . . Manifestum est autem quod nullus potest promoveri in aetatem perfectam, nisi primo fuerit natus, et similiter nisi primo aliquis fuerit baptizatus, non potest sacramentum confirmationis accipere." *Summa Theologica,* Pars III, q. 72, a. 6. Cf. Sainte-Beuve, p. 307; Blat, III, pars I, n. 81.

[3] ". . . si aliquis non baptizatus confirmaretur, nihil reciperet." *Summa Theologica,* Pars III, q. 72, a. 6. Cf. Blat, *loc. cit.*

The conferral of confirmation would have to be repeated after the subject had become validly baptized. As a matter of fact, until a person has first received baptism, he is not capable of receiving any of the sacraments.[4] For the reception of baptism is by divine institution the means of entrance into the Church, and the title to a reception of the other sacraments.[5] An unbaptized person therefore cannot be validly confirmed, since he has not been initiated into the Christian mysteries, or incorporated into the mystic body of Christ, which initiation or incorporation confers the right to receive the other sacraments.[6]

Obviously an instance wherein confirmation has been conferred upon one not validly baptized is not a case in which the doctrine of the reviviscence of the sacraments would have application. For this doctrine applies only when a sacrament has been validly but unfruitfully received, so that when the disposition is acquired, the absence of which had constituted an obstacle to the reception of the sacrament, the grace of the sacrament is said to revive.[7] Consequently this process of reviviscence would suppose in every case that the subject had been validly baptized and therefore was capable of receiving the other sacraments.[8]

What conclusion must be drawn, then, in the case of someone approaching the sacrament of confirmation in good faith, unaware that because of the improper matter and form that was used, or because of a defective intention on the part of the minister, he

---

[4] Canon 737, § 1; Ferreres, II, n. 294.

[5] Canon 737, § 1; "Nisi quis renatus fuerit ex aqua et Spiritu Sancto, non potest introire regnum Dei."—John, III: 5; "Baptismus enim ex institutione sua est janua omnium sacramentorum. . . ." De Augustinis, *De Re Sacramentaria* (2. ed., 3 vols., Romae, 1889), I, p. 281 (to be referred to hereafter with the name of the author); Coronata, I, 103; King, "Confirmation without Previous Baptism by Water," *ER*, LXVI (1922), 79.

[6] Cf. St. Thomas, *Summa Theologica*, pars III, q. 68, a. 1; Augustine, *A Commentary on the New Code of Canon Law* (8 vols., Vol., IV, 3. ed., St. Louis: Herder, 1925), IV, 113 (to be referred to hereafter with the name of the author); King, *ibid.*, p. 76.

[7] The doctrine of the reviviscence of grace has not been defined by the Church, but it is commonly held by the theologians. Cf. Coronata, I, nn. 34-37; Tanquerey, *Synopsis*, III, 386-391; Ferreres, II, n. 298.

[8] Cf. King, *ibid.*, p. 83.

had been baptized invalidly? From what has already been said it is evident that confirmation would not be received. For the deficiency resulting from the absence of baptism by water could not be supplied by the baptism of desire, insofar as the reception of other sacraments is concerned.[9]

Only the baptism of water renders the subject capable of receiving the other sacraments.[10] For the baptism of desire and the baptism of blood are not sacraments in the proper sense of the term, for they do not partake of the nature of a sign. They are sacraments only in a figurative sense, in that like baptism, properly so called, they effect the soul's justification.[11]

Would then the right intention and the fervent dispositions of the subject avail for nothing? There is a theory consonant with accepted theological principles that one who receives a sacrament invalidly, but in good faith and with suitable dispositions, will obtain from God certain extra-sacramental graces, much like those he would have received in the sacrament had it been validly received.[12] For God is not limited to the sacraments in the dispensing of His graces.[13] Nor is it consistent with His justice and mercy to permit good dispositions to go unrewarded. The graces received

---

[9] "Baptismus flaminis est baptismus desiderii, quod implicite continetur in actu caritatis Dei vel contritionis perfectae, qui quasi flatu Spiritu Sancti infunditur. Baptismus sanguinis est martyrium, i.e. mortis vel mortalis passionis perpessio pro fide aut alia virtute christiana."—Regatillo, I, n. 33. Baptism of blood would be almost entirely out of the question in this case. Cf. Coronata, I, n. 102.

[10] Canon 737, § 1; "Verum id discriminis inter sacramentum baptismi et inter baptismum sanguinis et baptismum flaminis intercedit: solum baptismi sacramentum reddit hominem aliorum sacramentorum capacem." Lehmkuhl, II, n. 57; Regatillo, *loc. cit.*

[11] "Sacramentum habet rationem signi; alia vero duo conveniunt cum baptismo aquae, non quidem quantum ad rationem signi, sed quantum ad effectum baptismatis; et ideo non sunt sacramenta." St. Thomas, *Summa Theologica,* Pars III, q. 66, a. 11, ad 2; Cappello, I, n. 110; Regatillo, *loc. cit.*

[12] Cf. "Can an Unbaptized Person Validly Receive Confirmation?" *ER,* XCII (1935), 192-195.

[13] "Dicendum quod virtus divina non est alligata sacramentis. Unde potest conferri homini spirituale robur ad confitendum publice fidem Christi absque sacramento confirmationis. . . ." St. Thomas, *Summa Theologica,* Pars III, q. 72, a. 6, ad 1.

in this case would probably be less abundant than if the sacrament had been received, but more abundant than the person's good dispositions would of themselves call for.[14]

Although the previous reception of baptism is an indispensable requirement for the valid reception of confirmation, that requirement would be fulfilled even if baptism had been received in a heretical sect, so long as the essential elements of matter, form and intention were properly observed.[15] This is evident from the teaching of the Church and from the practice of not rebaptizing heretics who enter the Church when it is clear that their previous baptism was correctly administered.[16]

The fact of a previous valid baptism is the only prerequisite for the valid confirmation of infants and of the perpetually insane who have never enjoyed the use of reason. These latter are equivalent to infants insofar as the law is concerned.[17] An additional demand is made upon adults, however. The adult, inasmuch as he possesses the use of reason, is required to have an intention to receive the sacrament, in order that he may be validly confirmed. The fundamental reason necessitating this condition is that, in the present order of divine providence, God does not permit creatures who enjoy the use of their faculties of intellect and will to become justified or sanctified apart from their consenting to His designs in their regard.[18] Moreover, some positive action on the part of the subject's will is necessary, in order to eliminate the possible presence of any impediment on the part of the will that would be opposed to the reception of the sacrament.[19] Accordingly, as is generally admitted, a state of neutrality or indiffer-

---

[14] "Can an Unbaptized Person validly Receive Confirmation?" *ER,* XCII (1935), 195; Pesch, *Praelectiones Dogmaticae* (9 vols., Friburgi Brisgoviae, 1894-1899), VI, n. 823 (to be referred to hereafter with the name of the author).

[15] Conc. Trident., sess. VII, can. 4: "Si quis dixerit, baptismum qui etiam datur ab haereticis in nomine Patris, et Filii, et Spiritus Sancti, cum intentione faciendi quod facit Ecclesia, non esse verum Baptismum: A.S."—Denzinger, *Enchiridion,* n. 860.

[16] Ferreres, II, n. 294.

[17] Canon 88, § 3; Aertnys-Damen, II, n. 31; Cappello, I, n. 72.

[18] Cappello. I, n. 73; Regatillo, I, 28.

[19] Cappello, *loc. cit.*

ence towards the reception of confirmation would be inadequate, and would render the conferral of the sacrament invalid.[20]

An intention is not required of infants and of the perpetually insane who have never experienced the use of reason, for they are incapable of performing wilful actions. An intention is required on the part of those individuals who have become victims of insanity after once having known the normal use of their faculties. The normal adult, inasmuch as he possesses the use of reason, is required to have an intention to receive the sacrament in order that he may be validly confirmed. Similarly, the insane person must have possessed such an intention before he lapsed into insanity, so that he can validly receive the sacrament.[21] In the case of infants and the perpetually insane the will of the minister who is acting in the name of Christ and of the Church is sufficient, so that Christ and the Church may be said to supply the intention for them.[22] The practice prevailing in the Church since its very inception renders the truth of this assertion beyond question.[23]

Since on the part of adults an intention to receive confirmation is necessary for its valid reception, it follows that any state of mind that would exclude the presence of this intention would cause the subject to be incapable of being confirmed. Consequently, if anyone inwardly repudiated the sacrament's conferral, or made only an outward pretense of receiving it, he would not be validly confirmed.[24] But how should one regard the case of a recipient who has exhibited apparently contrary intentions, so that it does not appear evident whether he has decided affirmatively or negatively?[25] Problems of this type are to be solved through a determination of which was the predominating intention.[26] The dispositions of soul which the person has manifested should ordinarily indicate which was the prevailing intention. But if such a con-

---

[20] Aertnys-Damen, II, n. 32; Cappello, *loc. cit.;* Coronata, I, n. 89; Regatillo, *loc. cit.*

[21] Regatillo, *loc. cit.*

[22] Cappello, *loc. cit.;* Regatillo, *loc. cit.*

[23] Regatillo, *loc. cit.*

[24] Cappello, *loc. cit.*

[25] Cappello, I, n. 75.

[26] Vermeersch, III, n. 167.

clusion cannot be securely reached, then the conferral of the sacrament should be conditioned upon the subject's having the necessary intention.[27]

A question of considerable practical consequence is the kind of intention that the recipient is obliged to have. Intentions considered in themselves differ from one another insofar as they are present or absent when the action is being performed; inasmuch as they are, or are not, accompanied by attention directed to the intention itself; and, insofar as they influence or do not influence the action which is taking place. Accordingly an actual intention is one which is here and now elicited and which is clearly adverted to while the action is being performed.[28] An intention is said to be virtual if it exists here and now and actually brings about the performance of the action, but is not adverted to while the action is taking place. If an intention is once made and never retracted, but in a particular action is not thought of, or has no positive influence in the performance of the human act as such, then it is called habitual. Such an intention could be by one in a state of unconsciousness. This habitual intention is explicit if the resulting action had been intended in itself; it is implicit when the action had been intended not in itself but in something else.[29] For example, the will to become a Christian includes the intention to receive baptism, which is a necessary step in becoming a Christian.[30] An interpretative intention is one improperly so called. It did not previously exist, nor does it have existence now, but it can be conjectured that it would have existed if the person had thought of the object or action in question.[31]

If with reference to the reception of confirmation the subject has an intention that adequately precludes the presence of any contrary disposition of the will, so that it can be said that he is receiving the sacrament not in opposition to but in harmony with his own will in the matter, then a valid conferral of the sacrament ensues. This condition is verified in the presence of a habitual in-

---

[27] Cappello, *loc. cit.*

[28] Cappello, I, n. 39; Coronata, I, 53.

[29] Coronata, *loc. cit.;* Cappello, *loc. cit.;* Regatillo, I, n. 14.

[30] Merkelbach, III, n. 94.

[31] Jone, n. 450; Vermeersch, III, n. 165; Coronata, *loc. cit.*

tention, even an implicit one, and accordingly proves adequate for the valid reception of confirmation.[32]

The element of attention which is a part of an actual intention is not necessary, since it is an act which proceeds solely from the intellect, and not also jointly from the will.[33] A virtual intention is likewise not essential, since the question is not that of the subject's conferring of the sacrament, but rather of his freely accepting a benefit which is bestowed by the minister of the sacrament.[34] On the other hand, an interpretative intention would be inadequate, since it involves no real action on the part of the will.[35]

The sufficiency of an implicit habitual intention is a factor of far-reaching import, since it implies the possibility of administering confirmation to someone even though he be unconscious, and in consequence thereof cannot at the moment give evidence of his intention. In such a case it may be possible to deduce, from what is known of the person's ordinary manner of living, the existence of a habitual intention on his part to receive confirmation. This intention would be implicit in a man's will of living and dying as a Catholic.[36] If the minister can with a degree of moral certainty assume the presence of an adequate intention, he should confer the sacrament absolutely, since a just cause is required for attaching a condition to the conferral of a sacrament, and evidently no such cause would be present in the case.[37] However, in the face of information that gives rise to a prudent doubt whether the subject really has a proper intention, due reverence for the sacrament would require that the administration of the sacrament be made dependent for its efficacy upon the presence of an intention that suffices for the valid reception.[38]

---

[32] Regatillo, I, n. 28; Cappello, I, n. 73.

[33] Regatillo, I, n. 20.

[34] Cappello, I, 73.

[35] Regatillo, I, n. 28.

[36] "Pro confirmatione sufficit *habitualis implicita* iuxta communem sententiam, contenta in voluntatem Catholice vivendi et moriendi." Regatillo, I, n. 28; cf Merkelbach, III, n. 94; Ferreres, II, n. 296.

[37] Vermeersch, III, n. 168.

[38] Vermeersch, *loc. cit.*

No other conditions besides the fact of a previous valid baptism on the part of all recipients, and the presence of a due intention on the part of adults, are required for the valid reception of confirmation. Not any of the sacraments requires moral probity as a condition essential for its validity, and only in the sacrament of penance is faith postulated as a necessary factor.[39]

ARTICLE 2. FOR THE LICIT AND FRUITFUL RECEPTION OF THE SACRAMENT

A valid but unfruitful reception of the sacrament of confirmation implies, on the one hand, the recipient's acquiring of the character of the sacrament, but, on the other hand, connotes his forfeiting of the graces that are destined to accompany the bestowal of that character.[40] In order to reap a licit and fruitful reception of confirmation the subject has to comply with conditions over and above such as are postulated for the valid reception. The first of these requirements is adherence to the Catholic belief.[41]

Although anyone properly baptized is capable of receiving confirmation, it is expressly forbidden by Church law to administer the sacraments to heretics and schismatics, even if they request them in good faith, unless they first have rejected their errors and become reconciled with the Church.[42] This prohibition is founded

[39] Faith is required for the valid reception of the sacrament of penance, since the contrition which itself is essential to this sacrament presupposes faith in the subject. Cf. Cappello, I, n. 69; Coronata, I, n. 87; Ferreres, II, n. 294.

[40] Coronata, I, n. 172; Marc-Gestermann-Raus, II, n. 1500.

[41] Regatillo, I, n. 85.

[42] Canon 731, § 2. Vetitum est Sacramenta Ecclesiae ministrare haereticis aut schismaticis, etiam bona fide errantibus eaque petentibus, nisi prius, erroribus reiectis, Ecclesiae reconciliati fuerint.

It is to be noted that the question debated by canonists regarding the licitness of conditionally conferring the "*necessary*" sacraments of penance and extreme unction to formal and material heretics and schismatics destitute of their senses, and to material heretics and schismatics not destitute of their senses, but at the point of death, and contrite and ready to do whatever is necessary for their salvation, has no bearing upon the consideration of the licit reception of confirmation. The lawfulness of conditionally conferring the sacraments of penance and of extreme unction derives solely on the fact that the administration of the sacraments was entrusted by Christ to the Church, and accordingly only those who belong to the body of this Church can be permitted to receive them.[43]

It is obvious that the Church cannot, as a rule, permit the sacraments to be administered to non-Catholics. Such a concession would amount to a betrayal of the Church's sacred trust and to a denial of its basic principles. The Catholic Church is the one Church commissioned by Christ to teach the way of salvation and to make available the sacraments, the means of salvation, to its members.[44] Membership in the Church is open to all who are prepared to live according to its teaching, and with membership in the Church comes the right to partake of its sacraments. To bestow its choicest blessings upon those who are unwilling to become members of the Church would cause scandal and promote religious indifference.[45]

An additional necessity for a licit and fruitful reception of confirmation is the state of grace. Confirmation is a sacrament of the living designed to bestow an increase to the grace that is presumed to be already present in the soul.[46] Should one who is about to receive the sacrament not be in possession of this requisite disposition, he could recover the state of grace either by means of a

---

from the desirability of producing the state of grace in the recipients. Consequently there would not be any justification for the administering of confirmation, in the event that the minister had the faculty to do so, since confirmation is a sacrament of the living. For its licit conferral the state of grace is a factor to be presupposed as already existing in the subject. Cf. Vermeersch-Creusen, *Epitome Iuris Canonici* (6. ed., 3 vols., Mechliniae-Romae: H. Dessain, 1937-1946), II, n. 16 (henceforth to be cited as *Epitome*); Pruemmer, *Manuale Iuris Canonici* (4. and 5. ed., Friburgi Brisgoviae: Herder, 1927), p. 369 (henceforth to be cited as *Manuale*); Wernz-Vidal, IV, pars I, n. 25; Augustine, *A Commentary on the New Code of Canon Law* (8 vols., Vol. IV, 3. ed., St. Louis: Herder, 1925), pp. 21-22 (henceforth to be referred to with the name of the author); Cappello, I, n. 62; Regatillo, I, n. 23; Coronata, I, n. 72; "Administration of the Sacraments to Dying Non-Catholics," *ER*, LXXXIV (1931), 296-297.

[43] Cappello, I, 62; Regatillo, I, n. 23.

[44] Woywod, I, n. 624.

[45] Regatillo, *loc. cit.*

[46] Cf. Coronata, I, n. 172; Ferreres, II, n. 361; Gury, n. 271; Wernz-Vidal, IV, pars I, n. 56; Marc-Gestermann-Raus, II, n. 1500.

sacramental confession, or by means of an elicited act of perfect sorrow for his sins.[47]

Although confession is regarded by some authors as being the more desirable means for obtaining this end,[48] the Code affords the liberty to choose either method, and consequently the necessity of confession as a prerequisite for the reception of confirmation could not be insisted upon in particular legislation. Such a law would in all likelihood be regarded by the faithful as implying a grave obligation.[49] A bishop could licitly exhort his subjects to have their sins absolved in confession before they receive confirmation, but he could not impose this practice by way of general law. Consequently, wherever diocesan statutes and conciliar decrees to this effect are in existence, they are not to be looked upon as imposing any obligation.[50]

Despite the fact that confirmation is a sacrament of the living, it is likely that its reception would avail for the remission of mortal sin in the event that someone not in the state of grace approached the sacrament in good faith and with sentiments of attrition.[51] However, if mortal sin were coupled with bad faith in the recipient of the sacrament, then a sacrilegious reception would be the result. Nevertheless the graces that would have accompanied a fruitful reception will revive once the subject has acquired the state of grace.[52]

Those whose reception of the sacrament would be illicit and unfruitful in consequence of the presence of grave sin on their souls should as a rule be denied the reception of confirmation. A refusal to administer the sacraments to those who are unworthy of it is demanded by reason of the reverence that is due the sacrament, in view of the minister's obligatory fidelity to his sacred trust, and in consideration of the virtue of charity which forbids the minister either to co-operate in the sin of the recipient or to allow an occasion for scandal.[53] However, the minister of con-

---

[47] Coronata, *loc. cit.;* Ferreres, *loc. cit.*

[48] Cf. Ferreres, II, n. 297; Cappello, I, n. 206.

[49] Coronata, *loc. cit.;* Cappello, *loc. cit.*

[50] Coronata, *loc. cit.;* Cappello, *loc. cit.*

[51] Coronata, *loc. cit.;* Blat, III, pars I, n. 81.

[52] Coronata, *loc. cit.;* Ferreres, II, n. 298.

[53] Cf. Regatillo, I, n. 22.

firmation is not required to investigate the worthiness of those who aspire to receive the sacrament. When a person presents himself as a candidate for confirmation, his worthiness is to be presumed, unless the opposite is clearly evident.[54] Evidence of unworthiness would surely be present in the case of public sinners,[55] of such as have contracted a censure of excommunication,[56] and of such upon whom there rests a personal interdict.[57]

A licit and fruitful reception of confirmation demands that the subject be sufficiently instructed.[58] The degree of religious knowledge that is to be required must be measured in its relation to the fact that the sacrament should normally be received at about the age of seven, and that its reception should precede that of first Holy Communion.[59] Accordingly, in keeping with the child's capacity for comprehension, a knowledge of the rudiments of faith, especially of those mysteries which are necessary as a means to salvation, should be possessed by the recipient. When the child has absorbed this information and has acquired an understanding of the meaning and of the effects of confirmation that proves adequate for making the desire to receive this sacrament, then it may be said that the requirement of sufficient instruction is duly met.[60] Those truths the knowledge of which is indispensable to salvation are the existence of God, the fact that He will eternally reward the good and punish the evil, and the mysteries of the Trinity and of the Incarnation.[61]

There should not be any difficulty in securing a desire on the part of the child to receive confirmation if he is made to realize

---

[54] Regatillo, *loc. cit.*

[55] Cappello, I, n. 63; Wernz-Vidal, IV, pars I, n. 56.

[56] Canon 2260, § 1; Wernz-Vidal, *loc. cit.;* Pistoni, n. 23.

[57] Canon 2275, § 2; Wernz-Vidal, *loc. cit.;* Pistoni, *loc. cit.*

[58] Canon 786.

[59] Canon 788; Pistoni, n. 23.

[60] Pistoni, *loc. cit.;* Merkelbach, III, n. 190; Dens, p. 236.

[61] Although it is a disputed point that a knowledge of the doctrines of the Trinity and of the Incarnation is indispensably necessary for salvation, there can be no question that some acquaintance with these mysteries should be imparted to those who approach the reception of confirmation, since these truths are so fundamental to the faith. Cf. Davis, I, 276-277; Cappello, I, 410; Kenrick, *Baptism, Also a Treatise on Confirmation,* p. 233.

that, while in the Holy Eucharist he is to receive our Lord, in the sacrament of confirmation he is through the Holy Ghost to receive the honor of being made a soldier of Christ. It should be brought home to the child that if he co-operates with the graces of confirmation, his faith in Christ and in His Church will always be characterized by a noble manliness through which he will transcend all human respect and rise above all human fears.[62]

Since it is according to the mind of the Church that children should be confirmed, make their first confession, and receive their first Holy Communion within a brief period of time, it should be possible to co-ordinate the instructions requisite for the reception of each of these sacraments. Accordingly, the plan of Cardinal Gasparri's catechism, which treats of the sacraments of confirmation, of penance and of the Holy Eucharist in connection with the truths indispensably necessary for salvation and other fundamentals of Christian doctrine, can serve as a useful means in providing an integrated course of instructions to children who are preparing for the reception of these three sacraments.[63]

A more detailed knowledge of Christian doctrine should be exacted from those who are beyond the normal age for the reception of confirmation.[64]

The ancient custom of fasting as a preparation for the reception of confirmation has fallen into desuetude, and now no longer receives mention in the Code.[65] The departure from this practice is accounted for by the fact that confirmation is now generally administered in the afternoon. To require the subject to remain fasting until that time would be to impose a grave hardship.[66] It is certain that an obligation to retain the custom of fasting does not exist by common law, nor could a bishop revive this ancient practice by means of a law that would be gravely binding.[67] However, when confirmation is administered in the morning, it re-

---

[62] Cf. Vermeersch-Creusen, *Epitome*, II, n. 65.

[63] Cf. Pistoni, n. 23.

[64] Pistoni, *loc. cit.;* Kenrick, *op. cit.*, n. 12.

[65] Ferreres, II, n. 361; Gury, n. 271.

[66] Cf. Coronata, I, n. 172.

[67] Coronata, *loc. cit.;* Cappello, I, n. 206; Merkelbach, III, n. 193.

mains a laudable practice to dispose oneself by fasting for a more worthy reception.[68]

ARTICLE 3. FOR COMPLIANCE WITH THE RITUALISTIC REQUIREMENTS

Canon 789. *Confirmandi, si plures sint, adsint primae manuum impositioni seu extensioni, nec nisi expleto ritu discedant.*

Canon 793. *Ex vetustissimo Ecclesiae more, ut in baptismo, ita etiam in confirmatione adhibendus est patrinus, si haberi possit.*

The ceremonies of the Church are the accidental or non-essential rites that are used in the solemn administration of the sacraments.[69] These ceremonies serve a manifold purpose. They contribute to the beauty and majesty of divine worship and promote reverence for the sacraments. When holy things are dispensed in a holy manner, greater reverence is thereby excited in the minister, in the recipients, and in the bystanders.[70] Moreover, the ceremonies vividly represent the efficacy of the sacraments in such a way as to impress the sacramental doctrine upon the minds of the faithful.[71] At the same time these liturgical rites elevate the mind to a contemplation of divine things, while drawing the hearts of the people to elicit acts of faith and charity.[72] The beauty of the liturgy is one of the Church's great heritages, and the faithful observance of the rubrics is one of the ways in which Catholics are distinguished from heretics, who, in general, employ but a minimum of liturgical ceremonies.[73]

In the light of these considerations it is evident that the minister of confirmation is bound to observe the ceremonies that are connected with the conferral of the sacrament. Even the ceremonies that are not necessary for the sacrament's validity may not be changed or omitted without a sufficiently just reason.[74]

---

[68] Cf. Cappello, *loc. cit.;* Dens, p. 236.
[69] Merkelbach, III, n. 104.
[70] Merkelbach, III, n. 105.
[71] Merkelbach, *loc. cit.*
[72] Merkelbach, *loc. cit.*
[73] Merkelbach, *loc. cit.*
[74] Merkelbach. III, n. 106.

In the administration of the sacrament of confirmation some of the rubrics that are employed are not essential to the sacrament. Among these are the imposition or the extension of hands which takes place at the beginning of the ceremony when the bishop invokes the Holy Ghost for the imparting of his seven-fold gift upon the recipients. This imposition of hands is not demanded for the valid conferral of the sacrament, since it is clear that the essential imposition of hands is that which is joined with the anointing of the recipient as performed by the bishop.[75]

This first imposition of hands does not form a part of the rite of confirmation as administered in the Oriental Church, and yet there is no question of the valid character of the sacrament when it is thus dispensed.[76] Moreover, in a response emanating from the Holy See it was stated that confirmation was not to be repeated conditionally in the case of those faithful who had failed to be present for the initial extension of hands, but who had later presented themselves for the conferral of the sacrament.[77] Consequently one could be validly confirmed without having been present for this initial ceremony. Nevertheless it is mandatory by reason of Church law that those who are about to receive confirmation are to be present when this first extension of hands takes place.[78]

The bishop therefore should not countenance a candidate's absenting himself from this ceremony. Could any just reason exist which would warrant an exception to this rule? One could imagine a case in which an adult convert, for example, is scheduled to be among a group of recipients of confirmation. However, on the day on which the ceremony is to take place it so happens that he is unavoidably detained and arrives after the initial ceremony has been completed, but in due time to partake in the essential

---

[75] Cf. Lennerz, *De Sacramento Confirmationis* (Romae: Pontificia Universitas Gregoriana, 1945), nn. 117-118; Lahousse, *Tractatus de Sacramentis in Genere, de Baptismo, de Confirmatione, et de Eucharistia* (Brugis, 1900), *De Confirmatione,* art. II, n. 7; Genicot-Salsmans, II, n. 160; Blat, III, pars I, n. 84.

[76] Genicot-Salsmans, *loc. cit.*

[77] S. C. de Prop. Fide (C. P. pro Sin.), 6 aug. 1840—*Fontes,* n. 4782; Genicot-Salsmans, *loc. cit.*

[78] Canon 789.

rites. Should he be permitted then to receive confirmation, or should he be required to defer his reception until a later date?

In judging whether a ceremony may be omitted either in itself, or in so far as an individual is concerned, one should advert to two factors. The first of these is the importance of that particular rubric to signify the effect or purpose of the sacrament, and the second is the scandal that is likely to ensue as a result of the ceremony's omission.[79] Now, of all the ceremonies linked with the rite of confirmation, the first extension of hands is the one which best symbolizes the conferral of the fullness of the Holy Ghost, which is the effect proper to this sacrament.[80] Secondly, since the vast majority of the faithful would hardly be able to distinguish the essential from the non-essential ceremonies, the dispensing of any candidate from partaking in this most impressive rite would cause at least undue astonishment.

Moreover, the recipient himself would probably be edified and impressed if the bishop insisted that the rubrics be completely observed in his case, even though he would be caused some inconvenience thereby. Consequently it appears that nothing short of a gravely urgent reason, such as the probability that another opportunity to receive confirmation would not be had, or would not be had for a considerable period of time, would justify a departure from this rule.

The happiest solution of this given case would be for the bishop to repeat the ceremony on behalf of this individual, on the assumption, of course, that the candidate has not been allowed to present himself for the essential ceremony. The ceremonies of confirmation are comparatively brief, and a single repetition of them should not cause the bishop considerable inconvenience.

To take one's leave from the scene of the ceremony before the complete rite has taken place would be to exhibit extremely poor taste and to evidence disrespect for the sacrament. Evidently only illness or some other serious reason could qualify as a sufficient warrant for taking this action.

---

[79] Merkelbach, III, n. 106.

[80] "Hic ritus, in quo sub forma explicitiori ac solemniori ipsa sacramentalis impositio manuum contenta in signatione veluti praefiguratur, est inter omnes caeremonias maxime symbolica proprii effectus huius sacramenti."—Doronzo, p. 402. Cf. St. Thomas, *Summa Theologica,* Pars III, q. 84, a. 4, ad 2.

If after confirmation has been administered to a group of candidates, it is discovered that some of them have not been present for one or several of the non-essential ceremonies, it is certain that these have been validly confirmed, and there is no obligation to supply the missing rubrics.[81]

Another ritualistic requirement which is not necessary for the valid reception of confirmation, but which is nevertheless required by law, is the use of a sponsor provided that one can be obtained.[82] It is commonly held that this law is a gravely binding law.[83] This opinion is supported by a response of the Holy Office in reply to a request from a bishop who had asked that with a general faculty he be authorized to dispense with sponsors at confirmation. Even though the bishop explained that he found it extremely difficult to obtain sponsors and that the smallness of his churches occasioned added inconvenience whenever they could be employed, the Holy Office refused his petition, inasmuch as the obligation of having a sponsor was a grave one.[84]

Nevertheless there are some authors who doubt the seriousness of this obligation. They assert that in this matter there is prevalent today a milder discipline than that which obtained in former times, and that a change of attitude in this regard is reflected by the inclusion in canon 793 of the qualifying clause, *"si haberi possit."*[85] Evidently the requirement of having a sponsor for the recipient of confirmation does not urge as seriously as does the obligation of having a sponsor for the recipient of baptism,[86] for the sponsor at confirmation is to exercise the obligation he has contracted by

---

[81] Cf. S. C. de Prop. Fide (C. P. pro Sin.), 6 aug. 1840—*Fontes,* n. 4782.

[82] Canon 793.

[83] Cf. Marc-Gestermann-Raus, II, n. 1503; Ferreres, II, n. 362; St. Alphonsus, VI, n. 185; Kenrick, II, n. 10; Merkelbach, III, n. 195; Jone, n. 489.

[84] S.C.S. Off., instr. (ad Archiep. Portus Principis), 5 sept. 1877: "Verum Emis Dñis ea mens stetit huiusmodi rationes non adeo valere ut generalem de patrino adhibendo legem vincere possint, quam legem, excepto casu gravis et urgentis necessitatis, egregius Ecclesiae Doctor S. Alphonsus simpliciter tradit obligare, et quidem sub gravi, excepto casu quo patrinus haberi non posset."—*Fontes,* n. 1053. Cf. Woywod, I, n. 691.

[85] Cf. canon 793; Cappello, I, n. 210; Coronata, I, n. 177; Pistoni, n. 59.

[86] Cf. canon 762; Regatillo, I, n. 91.

reason of his office only in the event that the sponsor at baptism is remiss in his duties.[87]

In practice it seems preferable not to permit an exception to the rule of canon 793, except in the face of just and grave reasons. When a doubt exists regarding the sufficiency of the causes present, then it appears that the milder opinion could be safely followed.[88]

As is customary in many places, the subject to be confirmed may choose the name of a saint, a name other than the one he received in baptism, and this name will be conferred upon him by the bishop during the essential part of the ceremony. The choosing of an additional name, however, is not of obligation.[89]

Since the outward appearance of the recipients should be in keeping with and suggest the reverence which the sacrament itself calls for, it is evident that those who are about to be confirmed should be neatly and fittingly attired. Women especially are to be counselled to be modest and dignified in their appearance at their approach to the reception of this sacrament.[90]

---

[87] Ferreres, II, n. 362; Cappello, I, n. 212.

[88] Cf. canon 15.

[89] Cf. S. R. C., Iaurinen., 20 sept. 1749—*Fontes,* n. 5789; Merkelbach, III, n. 193.

[90] Cf. S. C. de Sacramentis, instr., 20 maii 1934—Bouscaren, II, 185-188.

CHAPTER IX

Conditions Required with Reference to the Time and Place for Confirmation

Article 1. The Time for the Conferring of Confirmation

Canon 790. *Hoc sacramentum quovis tempore conferri potest; maxime autem decet illud administrari in hebdomada Pentecostes.*

The present law of the Church regarding the time for the conferring of confirmation can be said to be the outcome of necessity and utility.[1] When the faithful were very small in number and confirmation was administered immediately after the conferral of baptism, the custom came into being of restricting the administration of these sacraments to the vigils of Easter and Pentecost.[2] In some places, the feasts of Christmas and Epiphany were added to the days on which these sacraments might be received.[3]

However, with the vastly increased numbers of the faithful, and with the departure from the practice of conferring the two sacraments on the same occasion, it became impossible to confine the administration of either sacrament to any definite day. This impossibility was verified almost to the same degree in the case of confirmation as it was in that of baptism, since every baptized person possessed of due intention was a potential recipient of confirmation.[4] Hence it came to be that the time for administering confirmation was left to the bishop's discretion. This custom prevails today, so that the sacrament may be conferred on any day, and at any hour of the day.[5]

---

[1] Doronzo, pp. 403-404.

[2] Cf. Duchesne, pp. 292-295; Doronzo, *loc. cit.;* Sainte-Beuve, p. 340.

[3] Doronzo, *loc. cit.;* Sainte-Beuve, *loc. cit.*

[4] Cf. canon 786; Regatillo, I, n. 85.

[5] Canon 790. Cf. Wernz-Vidal, IV, pars I, n. 59; Doronzo, *loc. cit.;* Piscetta-Gennaro, *Elementa Theologiae Moralis ad Codicem Iuris Canonici Exacta,* Vol. V (Torino: Società Editrice Internazionale, 1927), n. 255 (henceforth to be cited with the names of the authors).

Moreover, there is no intrinsic reason why confirmation cannot be administered on any day, for the conferral of this sacrament is not strictly incompatible with the liturgy of any feast, and no prohibition exists in the universal law that would rule out the bestowal of confirmation on any particular day.[6]

However, unless necessity would dictate otherwise, it would be preferable not to confirm subjects on the last three days of Holy Week, or during the time when penitential offices, or the offices of the dead, are being observed.[7]

Any hour of the day is suitable for receiving the sacrament of confirmation. It is not necessary that the sacrament be administered during the morning, in order that the subjects may observe the fast while receiving. Although such a practice was formerly in vogue,[8] there is no mention of it now in the Code, and its observance now is at most a matter of counsel.[9] Formerly it was also customary, whenever it could be done so conveniently, to administer the sacrament at the third hour of the day, in order to commemorate the hour at which the Holy Ghost descended upon the Apostles on the day of Pentecost.[10]

According to the present law, however, only one preference is stated by the Church as to the time for conferring confirmation. This preference is suggested in the wording of canon 790 to the effect that confirmation is most fittingly administered in Pentecost Week. The suitableness of this particular time derives from the fact that on the day of Pentecost the Holy Ghost descended upon the Apostles, and in his so doing demonstrated the nature and the effects of confirmation most vividly and strikingly.[11]

A way whereby there may be harmonized the two statements contained in canon 790 should be sought. The first statement

---

[6] Cf. Blat, III, pars I, n. 86.

[7] "Non expedit fideles confirmare in triduo maiore, vel tempore officiorum poenitentialium, seu defunctorum." Nabuco, *Pontificalis Romani Expositio Iuridico-Practica* (3 vols., Petropoli: Editôra Vozes Ltda., 1945), I, n. 45 (to be referred to hereafter with the name of the author).

[8] Cf. Council of Arles (1260), canon 3—Mansi, XXIII, 1004.

[9] Ferreres, II, n. 361; Gury, n. 271.

[10] Acts, II: 1-11; II, 16; S. C. de Prop. Fide, instr. 4 maii. 1774—*Fontes,* n. 4565; Sainte-Beuve, p. 340.

[11] Acts, II: 1-11; Blat, III, pars I, n. 86.

allows the bishop to choose the time of confirmation at his own discretion. The second statement points to the week of Pentecost as the most appropriate time for the conferring of this sacrament.

One method the bishop may employ in order to observe the demands of fittingness is to begin his confirmation tour by administering the sacrament in the Cathedral Church on Pentecost Sunday.[12] In this way the time of conferring the sacrament will be completely in harmony with the mind of the Church, and something will have been done by way of promoting a better understanding of the meaning of confirmation on the part of the faithful.

Another approach to a complete observance of canon 790 is to have the confirmation of men and women who are eligible for the reception of the sacrament take place on Pentecost Sunday and in the Cathedral Church of the diocese, rather than in the respective parish churches of these recipients.[13]

It is to be observed that the Church's statement of its preference for the week of Pentecost as the most suitable time for the conferring of confirmation does not thereby impose a grave obligation to make allowances for this preference in bestowing the sacrament upon the faithful.[14]

ARTICLE 2. THE PLACE FOR THE CONFERRING OF CONFIRMATION

Canon 791. *Licet proprius confirmationis administrandae locus ecclesia sit, ex causa tamen quam minister iustam ac rationabilem iudicaverit, potest hoc sacramentum in quolibet alio decenti loco conferri.*

The dignity befitting confirmation as a sacrament directs that the proper place for its administration be a church, inasmuch as a church is a sacred building dedicated to divine worship.[15]

---

[12] Cf. Wernz-Vidal, IV, pars I, n. 59.

[13] Cf. *Ninth Synod of the Diocese of Harrisburg* (*1943*), Appendix IV, n. 17.

[14] Wernz-Vidal, *loc. cit.*

[15] Canon 1161. Ecclesiae nomine intelligitur aedes sacra divino cultui dedicata eum potissimum in finem ut omnibus Christifidelibus usui sit ad divinum cultum publice exercendum. Cf. Blat, III, pars I, n. 87; Nabuco, I, n. 46.

In so far as the administration of confirmation is concerned, an oratory, whether public or semi-public, or even the private chapel of a cardinal or of a bishop, would be the equivalent of a church.[16] For although oratories are not erected especially with a view to enabling the faithful in general to practice public worship,[17] nevertheless, unless there are prescriptions of the liturgy to the contrary, all the sacred functions may be celebrated in a public oratory that under the authority of the Ordinary has been dedicated perpetually to public worship according to the norms which the Church has prescribed.[18]

Moreover, in legitimately erected semi-public oratories, all the divine offices and ecclesiastical functions may be celebrated so long as the rubrics do not dictate otherwise, and there is no prohibition on the part of the Ordinary to the contrary.[19] The same can be said of the chapels of cardinals and bishops, since these sacred places are endowed with the same rights and privileges that are given to semi-public oratories.[20] Furthermore there are no pre-

---

[16] Canon 1188, § 1. Oratorium est locus divino cultui destinatus, non tamen eo potissimum fine ut universo fidelium populo usui sit ad religionem publice colendam.

§ 2. Est vero oratorium:

1°. *Publicum,* si praecipue erectum sit in commodum alicuius collegii aut etiam privatorum, ita tamen ut omnibus fidelibus, tempore saltem divinorum officiorum, ius sit legitime comprobatum, illud adeundi;

2°. *Semi-publicum,* si in commodum alicuius communitatis vel coetus fidelium eo convenientium erectum sit, neque liberum cuique sit illud adire.

3°. *Privatum* seu *domesticum,* si in privatis aedibus in commodum alicuius tantum familiae vel personae privatae erectum sit. Cf. Blat, *loc. cit.;* Nabuco, *loc. cit.;* Cappello, I, n. 216.

[17] Cf. canon 1188.

[18] Canon 1191, § 2. Quare in oratorio publico, dummodo auctoritate Ordinarii ad publicum Dei cultum perpetuo per benedictionem vel consecrationem, ad normam can. 1155, 1156, dedicatum fuerit, omnes sacrae functiones celebrari possunt, salvo contrario rubricarum praescripto. Cf. Beste, *Introductio in Codicem* (2. ed., Collegeville: St. John's Abbey Press, 1944), p. 573 (to be cited hereafter with the name of the author).

[19] Canon 1193. In oratoriis semi-publicis legitime erectis, omnia divina officia functionesve ecclesiasticae celebrari possunt, nisi obstent rubricae aut Ordinarius aliqua exceperit.

[20] Canon 1189.

scriptions of the liturgy which forbid the conferral of confirmation in any of these types of oratory.[21]

Although the administration of confirmation forms a part of divine worship, and although this sacrament should ordinarily be conferred in a place set apart for the exercise of divine worship,[22] there can exist reasonable and just causes which will warrant the conferral of the sacrament even though an ideal place for so doing is not available.[23] The minister is the judge as to what circumstances will qualify as reasonable and just causes for providing persons with the sacrament in places other than a church or an oratory.[24] The illness of the subject, the smallness of the church, or its inaccessibility to some of his people, are causes that may well merit his consideration.[25] The conditions which prevail during a time of war present many instances wherein the minister becomes justified in using his powers to confirm, even though access to a church or to an oratory would be out of the question.[26] The locale which is used instead of the normal places for the conferring of confirmation should be sufficiently respectable that the sacrament will not be subjected to irreverence.[27]

It is held as the more common opinion that the minister is bound by a light obligation not to confer confirmation outside a church or an oratory, even though the place which is substituted is a respectable one, unless there is truly present a just cause for his doing so.[28] He is gravely bound not to administer the sacrament in an indecent place in the absence of any justifying cause.[29]

Scholion. The bishop's prerogative to administer confirmation in the exempt places of his diocese.

---

[21] Cf. Ayrinhac, *Administrative Legislation in the New Code of Canon Law* (London, New York, Toronto: Longmans, Green and Co., 1930), pp. 42-44 (hereafter cited with the name of the author).

[22] Cf. Ayrinhac, p. 7.

[23] Canon 791.

[24] Canon 791.

[25] Cf. Pistoni, n. 76; Coronata, I, 176.

[26] Pistoni, *loc. cit.*

[27] Cf. canon 791; Cappello, I, 216.

[28] Cf. Cappello, I, n. 216; Coronata, *loc. cit.*

[29] Cf. Cappello, *loc. cit.*; Coronata, *loc. cit.*

Canon 792. *Episcopo ius est intra fines suae dioecesis confirmationem administrandi in locis quoque exemptis.*

One of the functions intimately connected with the office of the bishop is his control over the administration of the sacraments in his diocese.[30] It is his duty to guard ecclesiastical discipline against abuse in regard to the conferral of the sacraments, as well as in other matters.[31] In keeping with this function it is natural that it should be his prerogative to administer confirmation in any place in the diocese.[32] Even exempt religious who along with their houses and churches are not subject to the jurisdiction of the bishop, except in those cases which are expressly mentioned in law,[33] must yield to the bishop's right in this matter. In fact, this right of the bishop is so fundamental, that he may confer confirmation in the churches of exempt regulars even contrary to their will, and should they attempt to impede him from doing so, he can proceed against them by means of canonical censures.[34]

This prerogative of bestowing confirmation in the exempt places of the diocese prevails, of course, only within the bounds of the bishop's own territory. If he wished to solemnly administer confirmation in a church of exempt religious in a diocese other than his own, he would need the consent of the religious superior in question, in addition to the at least reasonably presumed consent of the local ordinary.[35] It is true that by law the bishop has the right privately and without the use of crozier and mitre to confirm his own subjects in another diocese, even without securing the consent of the local ordinary.[36] However, this right would certainly not seem to allow him to make use of the church of an exempt religious institute for this purpose, should the religious be opposed to his doing so.

Those who rule the clergy and people of a district that is dis-

---

[30] Cf. canon 336, § 2; Beste, p. 267.

[31] Canon 336, § 2.

[32] Canon 792.

[33] Cf. canons 615; 618, § 1; Beste, pp. 417-420.

[34] Cf. S.C.C., *Brixien.*, 9 iul. 1657—*Fontes*, n. 2750.

[35] Cf. canon 337, § 1.

[36] Canon 783, § 2.

tinct from any diocese are called abbots and prelates *nullius*.[37] They possess the faculty of administering confirmation within the limits of their respective territories and during the time in which they hold office.[38] These prelates evidently enjoy in their abbacies or prelacies the same right which the bishop possesses in his diocese, namely of giving confirmation even in exempt places.[39] For the Code states that when the term "bishop" is employed in the law, the term is meant to apply to abbots and prelates *nullius* also, unless the opposite is clear from the nature of the case, or from the context.[40]

Vicars and prefects apostolic are those who govern territories which are not erected into dioceses.[41] Canon 792 seems also to apply to them as far as their respective territories are concerned, for they enjoy the faculty of conferring confirmation in the same manner as do abbots and prelates *nullius*.[42] Moreover, in the territories which they rule, they have the same rights and faculties which residential bishops possess, unless in particular cases the Holy See has imposed some restriction.[43]

---

[37] Cf. canon 319, § 1; Woywod, I, n. 236.

[38] Canon 782, § 3.

[39] Canon 792.

[40] Canon 215, § 2.—In iure nomine dioecesis venit quoque abbatia vel praelatura *nullius;* et nomine Episcopi, Abbas vel Praelatus *nullius,* nisi ex natura rei vel sermonis contextu aliud constet. Cf. Blat, III, pars I, n. 87.

[41] Cf. canon 293, § 1; Woywod, I, n. 223.

[42] Canon 782, § 3.

[43] Canon 294, § 1. Vicarii et Praefecti Apostolici iisdem iuribus et facultatibus in suo territorio gaudent quae in propriis dioecesibus competunt Episcopis residentialibus, nisi quid Apostolica Sedes reservaverit.

CHAPTER X

The Reception of Confirmation from a Minister Other Than a Bishop

Article 1. The Latin Priest with an Apostolic Indult

Canon 782, § 4. *Prebyter latini ritus cui, vi indulti, haec facultas competat, confirmationem valide confert solis fidelibus sui ritus, nisi in indulto aliud expresse cautum fuerit.*

The recipient of confirmation has been contemplated thus far without particular reference to the minister of the sacrament. Since, however, there exist particular questions involving the recipient of confirmation by reason of the possession by simple priests of the faculty to confirm, the ensuing pages will be devoted to a consideration of these questions and to a solution of them.

The bishop alone is the ordinary minister of confirmation.[1] The extraordinary minister is a priest to whom the faculty of confirming has been granted either by common law, or by special indult of the Holy See.[2]

A priest of the Latin rite who has been granted an indult to administer confirmation must be guided in the exercise of his faculty by the terms of the indult which he has received.[3] Moreover, it is to be understood that he cannot validly or lawfully use his faculty in favor of members of Oriental rites, unless by the wording of his indult he is expressly given the right to do so.[4] The indult which the priest receives may be either a personal indult or a local one.[5] In the former case the valid and lawful use of his faculty is restricted to the conferral of the sacrament in behalf of those persons who are mentioned in the indult.[6] In the latter case

[1] Canon 782, § 1; Coleman, pp. 60-72.

[2] Canon 782, § 2; Coleman, pp. 104-105.

[3] Cf. Aertnys-Damen, II, n. 87; Coronata, I, n. 167.

[4] Canon 782, § 4.

[5] Aertnys-Damen, *loc. cit.*

[6] Aertnys-Damen, *loc. cit.*

the valid and licit exercise of the priest's power to confirm is limited to the territory specified by the grant. Within this locality he can confirm the subjects of that territory, and also others not belonging to it, unless in the case of the latter there exists an express prohibition to the contrary on the part of their ordinary.[7] Should, however, the priest in this case confer confirmation upon subjects of another territory in spite of such a prohibition, his administration of the sacrament would be valid, but unlawful.[8]

An example of a local indult issued to certain priests empowering them to confer confirmation is had in the decree of the Sacred Congregation of the Sacraments, *Spiritus Sancti munera,* of September 14, 1946.[9] The pastors and other priests contemplated in this decree can validly and licitly confirm only those persons who are actually within their territory, although not to the exclusion of persons actually present in places not subject to the pastor's jurisdiction. These places would include seminaries, lodging places, hospitals, and other institutions, even those of religious, regardless of the manner in which they are exempt.[10] Outside the territory specified, however, the priests empowered to confirm cannot validly or licitly use their faculty.[11]

A further restriction is placed upon this faculty in that those in whose favor it is exercised must be in real danger of death from illness, from which it is foreseen that they will die.[12]

ARTICLE 2. THE ORIENTAL PRIEST WITH A SPECIAL PRIVILEGE

Canon 782, § 5. *Nefas est presbyteris ritus orientalis, qui facultate vel privilegio gaudent confirmationem una cum baptismo infantibus sui ritus conferendi, eandem ministrare infantibus latini ritus.*

The faithful of the Oriental Catholic Church, with the exception of the Maronites, generally receive confirmation as infants,

[7] Canon 784; Aertnys-Damen, *loc. cit.*

[8] Aertnys-Damen, *loc. cit.*

[9] *AAS,* XXXVIII (1946), 349; Zerba, n. 28.

[10] Cf. Hannan, "Decree on the Administration to Those in Danger of Death through Illness," *The Jurist,* VII (1947), p. 224; Pistoni, n. 102.

[11] Cf. Zerba, *loc. cit.*

[12] Cf. Hannan, *loc. cit.*

immediately after the reception of baptism and through the ministry of a simple priest.[13] Whenever the subject to be confirmed is an adult, and as a rule when confirmation has not been received at the time of baptism, the conferral of confirmation is reserved to the bishop.[14]

Priests of the Oriental rite, on the basis of faculties conceded either expressly or tacitly by the Holy See, validly and licitly confer confirmation together with baptism to children of their own rite, except in those places where their faculty to confirm has been expressly withdrawn.[15] The power to confirm was expressly revoked in the cases of the Oriental priests in Italy and its adjacent islands, in the Island of Cyprus, in Bulgaria, and from the priests of the Maronite rite.[16]

A priest of an Oriental rite who has the power of conferring confirmation together with baptism can exercise this faculty not only in favor of persons pertaining to his own rite, but also in behalf of subjects of a different rite, provided that in this latter rite the same privilege obtains regarding the administration of both sacraments.[17] This general rule would suffer an exception in cases wherein particular Oriental law would make provision to the contrary.[18]

This privilege does not prevail in the Latin rite, however, and the law of the Code makes it gravely illicit for Oriental priests to exercise their faculty of conferring confirmation upon members of the Latin rite.[19]

Would such a use of this faculty be not only gravely unlawful, but invalid as well? The point is disputed. The controversy centers about the significance of the word *"nefas"* of canon 782, § 5.[20]

---

[13] Cf. Cappello, I, n. 784; Coronata, I, n. 168; Coleman, p. 124.

[14] Cappello, *loc. cit.;* Coleman, *loc. cit.*

[15] Aertnys-Damen, II, n. 87; Cappello, *loc. cit.;* Coronata, I, n. 168.

[16] Cf. S.C.S. Off., 5 iul. 1853—*Fontes,* n. 924; Coleman, *loc. cit;* Cappello (*loc. cit.*) claims that this faculty was not withdrawn from the Greek priests of Bulgaria, but only from the Latin priests of that country.

[17] Cf. S.C.S. Off., instr. 22 apr. 1896—*Fontes,* n. 1178.

[18] Coleman, p. 129.

[19] Canon 782, § 5.

[20] Coleman, pp. 127-129; Blat, III, pars I, n. 76.

There is much to be said in favor of the opinion which interprets paragraph 5 of canon 782 as a prohibition of the divine law which would nullify the confirmation of a member of the Latin Church by a priest of an Oriental rite.[21]

In the first place, the bishop alone is the ordinary minister of confirmation.[22] It is maintained, furthermore, that he is such by reason of the divine law,[23] for the reasons that Scripture reveals that in the beginning only the Apostles were permitted to administer confirmation,[24] and that the Tradition of the Church has understood this fact to signify that as an ordinary power the ministry of confirmation is restricted by the divine law to the Apostles and their successors, the bishops.[25]

Priests are extraordinary ministers of the sacrament.[26] In order that they may validly administer confirmation they must receive delegation, and, regardless of what speculation may have previously existed as to the possibility of a bishop's commissioning a priest to confer confirmation,[27] as a practical rule it is certain that without delegation from the Holy Father no priest can now validly administer confirmation. Delegation received from a bishop would not suffice.[28]

In view of the fact that the ordinary power to administer confirmation is restricted by the divine law to bishops, and in consideration of the fact that it is the exclusive right of the Roman

---

[21] Cf. Blat, *loc. cit.*

For reasons to be set forth later, the writer feels constrained to reject this opinion in favor of the more common one, but before doing so, he would like to give the former an adequate presentation.

[22] Conc. Trident., Sess. VII, can. 3, *de confirmatione:* "Si quis dixerit, sanctae confirmationis ordinarium ministrum non esse solum episcopum, sed quemvis simplicem sacerdotem: A.S."—Denzinger, *Enchiridion,* n. 873; canon 782, § 1.

[23] Blat, *loc. cit.;* Doronzo, p. 391.

[24] Acts, VIII: 4-19; XIX: 1-6; Doronzo, *loc. cit.;* Pesch, VI, n. 544.

[25] Cf. Conc. Florent., *Decret. pro Armenis,* 22 nov. 1439—Denzinger, *Enchiridion,* n. 697; Doronzo, *loc. cit.*

[26] Canon 782, § 2.

[27] Cf. Pesch, VI, n. 556; Regatillo, I, n. 82.

[28] Coleman, p. 105; cf. St. Thomas, *Summa Theologica,* Pars III, q. 72, a. 11, ad 1; Doronzo, p. 394; Billot, *De Ecclesiae Sacramentis* (7. ed., 2 vols., Romae: Pontificia Universitas Gregoriana, 1931), I, 307-309.

Pontiff to delegate priests to confirm, it seems that the word *"nefas,"* which in itself signifies only a strong prohibition, is equivalent in this case to both a prohibition of the divine law and to a withholding of the jurisdiction needed for the valid conferral of the sacrament.[29]

Canon 782, § 5, accordingly appears to contain an invalidating law according to the rule of canon 11.[30]

One of the arguments which Coleman uses in favor of the opposite opinion is that the word *"nefas"* as used elsewhere in the Code denotes nothing more than a prohibition.[31] He states that although *"nefas"* is used in canon 817 to prohibit the consecration of the bread without the wine, or vice versa, and to prohibit the consecration of both outside the celebration of Mass, it is commonly held that the consecration of one element without the other, or the consecration of both outside Mass, is possible.[32]

However, this does not appear to be a valid argument, for the common opinion relative to this instance is opposed by no less an authority than Lugo,[33] just as in the controversy that is here being considered the common opinion is not accepted by such a reputable canonist as Blat.[34]

However, although this view has much appeal to the writer, he rejects it in favor of the common opinion that confirmation of persons of the Latin rite by Oriental priests is illicit, but nevertheless valid. Cappello argues in favor of the common view that invalidity is to be admitted when it is evident either from the nature of things or from Apostolic prescription; but that in this case invalidity is not demonstrated from either of these sources.[35]

---

[29] Cf. Blat, III, pars I, n. 76.

[30] Canon 11. Irritantes aut inhabilitantes eae tantum leges habendae sunt, quibus aut actum esse nullum aut inhabilem esse personam expresse vel aequivalenter statuitur.

[31] *The Minister of Confirmation*, pp. 127-128.

[32] *Ibid.*, p. 127.

[33] Disp. XX, n. 104, apud Tanquerey, *Synopsis*, III, n. 870. Lugo held that the Eucharist as a sacrament cannot be separated from the Eucharist as a sacrifice, and for the latter concept the consecration of both species is required.

[34] *Loc. cit.*

[35] Cf. Cappello, I, n. 199; Coronata, I, 168; Aertnys-Damen, II, n. 87; Piscetta-Gennara, V, n. 241; Woywod, I, n. 683; Coleman, pp. 124-130; Vermeersch, III, n. 243; Regatillo, I, n. 82; Merkelbach, III, n. 187.

A factor which seems to make the common opinion the more probable one is the constant policy which the Sacred Congregations have maintained in dealing with cases of Latin Catholics who have received confirmation from priests of Oriental rites. From a consideration of the decisions in which this policy is revealed, it does not seem likely that the Holy See would have intended canon 782, § 5, to be an invalidating law.

In responding to petitions as to what procedure should be followed in these instances, the replies of the Sacred Congregations have been substantially the same; viz., that it is not expedient that these subjects be reconfirmed by the bishop, unless there is a question of their being promoted to tonsure or orders, or either the subjects themselves or their parents request it, in which cases the sacrament should be conferred secretly and conditionally.[36]

These responses do not settle the question of the validity of these administrations of confirmation. It may be that the Holy See looks upon such conferrals as most probably invalid. In this hypothesis it may be that a general policy of readministering confirmation conditionally would not be deemed expedient, because confirmation is not absolutely necessary for salvation. However, those approaching tonsure and orders would have to be reconfirmed, since the reception of confirmation is required for the licit reception of orders.[37] As to those who request the sacrament for themselves or for their children, a certainly valid administration of confirmation in place of one probably invalid would have to be granted to those making such a request.[38]

It seems more likely that the Holy See looks upon these conferrals as most probably valid. This being so, a general policy of readministering confirmation is not expedient. However,

[36] Cf. S. C. de Prop. Fide (C. G.), 5 iul. 1886, ad 2. . . . "Non expedire ut confirmati de quibus in casu, iterum ab Episcopo inungantur, nisi ad tonsuram et ordines promovendi sunt . . . quibus in casibus Confirmationis sacramentum secreto conferatur et sub conditione."—*Fontes,* n. 4915. Cf. S.C.S. Off., litt. 16 mart. 1872—*Fontes,* n. 1021; S.C.S. Off. (Ierosolym.), 14 ian. 1885—*Fontes,* n. 1090; Cappello, I, n. 199.

[37] Canon 974, § 1, 1°.

[38] Canon 785, § 1—Episcopus obligatione tenetur sacramentum hoc subditis rite et rationabiliter petentibus conferendi, praesertim tempore visitationis dioecesis.

for the reasons given above a certainly valid administration of confirmation is desirable for those approaching orders or tonsure,[39] as well as for those who reasonably petition the conferral of the sacrament.

Although the confirmation of a Latin Catholic by an Oriental Catholic priest is doubtfully valid, it has already been seen what norm is to be observed whenever a case of this type is encountered.*

A further difficulty may present itself. It relates to a doubt regarding the fact that confirmation was conferred. On this point a question was sent to the Sacred Congregation of the Propagation of the Faith. The query sought to ascertain whether, in the event that a child of the Latin rite was known to have been baptized by an Oriental priest, it should be presumed that the child was also confirmed, or whether confirmation should be repeated conditionally. The Sacred Congregation replied that recourse should be made in particular cases, and a complete description of the matter should be provided when the recourse is made.[40]

ARTICLE 3. THE SCHISMATIC PRIEST

Before the schism of Photius (815-897) priests of the Oriental Church possessed the faculty to administer confirmation.[41] During the course of the councils which were held in an effort to effect a return of the schismatics, the validity of the confirmation conferred by the priests who had fallen into schism was never questioned.[42]

It is true that this faculty was expressly withdrawn from Oriental priests, both Catholic and schismatic in Bulgaria, in Albania, in Italy and its adjacent islands, and from the Lebanon Maronites.[43] However, in view of the documents of the Sacred Congregations it appears that in the places where the faculty to confirm has not

---

[39] Canon 974, § 1, 1°.

*See footnote n. 36, page 123.

[40] S. C. de Prop. Fide (C. G.), 5 iul. 1886, ad 3—*Fontes,* n. 4915.

[41] Cf. Souarn, "De Presbytero Orientali Confirmationis Ministro," *Jus Pontificium* (Romae, 1921-1940), XI (1931), 137.

[42] Cf. Pesch, VI, n. 551.

[43] Cf. S.C.S. Off., 5 iul. 1853—*Fontes,* n. 924; Noldin-Schmitt, III, n. 89; Coleman, p. 55.

been revoked the schismatic priests enjoy the same power to validly administer confirmation as do the Oriental Catholic priests.[44]

When a repetition of confirmation is being contemplated in the case of persons previously confirmed by schismatic priests, usually there is proposed the same norm of action which obtains for the instances wherein there is being considered a reconfirmation of members of the Latin rite who had already been confirmed by Oriental Catholic priests. As has already been seen, the general rule for proceeding in these cases is that it is not expedient to repeat confirmation, unless there is question of the subject's advancing to tonsure or orders, or unless the subject or his parents request it, in which case the rite should be performed secretly and conditionally.[45]

In view of these responses it is probable that schismatic priests from whom the power to confirm has not been expressly revoked have the power of administering confirmation, despite opinions to the contrary.[46] The reason which one author gives for denying that schismatic priests have this power is that priests are extraordinary ministers of this sacrament, so that they possess the faculty to confer confirmation only when delegated to do so by the Roman Pontiff, who however is not to be thought of as being willing to concede this power to schismatics.[47]

According to this view the character of the responses of the Holy Office is accounted for by the fact that confirmation is not absolutely necessary for salvation.[48] However, this does not seem to be an adequate explanation.[49]

At any rate, although the problem of the validity of confirmation administered by schismatic priests has not been settled to the satisfaction of all, a set of rules for dealing with practical cases involving this problem may be derived from various responses of the Holy See.

---

[44] Cf. S.C.S. Off., 5 iul. 1853—*Fontes,* n. 924; S.C.S. Off., litt. 16 mart. 1872—*Fontes,* n. 1021; S.C.S. Off. (Ierosolym.), 14 ian. 1885—*Fontes,* n. 1090.

[45] Cf. documents cited in footnote n. 36, p. 123.

[46] Cf. Noldin-Schmitt, III, n. 89.

[47] Coronata, I, n. 168; cf. Cappello, I, 176.

[48] Coronata, *loc. cit.*

[49] Cf. Noldin-Schmitt, *loc. cit.*

The first rule is that when Latin Catholics, or schismatics who are returning to the unity of the Church, have received confirmation from schismatic priests of the places where the faculty to confirm has been expressly withdrawn, then confirmation should be administered to these subjects unconditionally.[50]

Secondly, if under the same circumstances the confirmation was conferred by a priest of a place where the faculty has not been expressly revoked, then it is not expedient to again confer the sacrament, unless the person involved is being advanced to tonsure or orders, unless he or his parents request it, or unless after an examination of the manner in which the sacrament was administered it is learned that the anointing was performed by means of a brush or some other instrument.[51] In these cases the sacrament should be repeated secretly and conditionally.[52]

Finally, if there is doubt concerning the place or the manner in which the sacrament was conferred, or if the case is attended with some other reasonable motive for uncertainty, then recourse to the Holy See should be had in particular cases.[53]

Although the foregoing observations are derived from responses which contemplated only the confirmation of Latin Catholics and schismatics by schismatic priests, there seems to be no reason why these norms may not also be applied to Oriental Catholics who received confirmation from schismatic priests. For if it is true, as the responses seem to indicate, that schismatic priests truly possess the faculty of administering confirmation from the Roman Pontiff, then particular Oriental law could prohibit the exercise of this faculty towards Oriental Catholics, but could not invalidate it. This consideration would assume a practical bearing for pastors of an Oriental rite whose subjects may have been confirmed by a schismatic priest, and for pastors of the Latin rite should Oriental Catholics thus confirmed decide to transfer to the Latin rite.[54]

---

[50] S.C.S. Off., 5 iul. 1853—*Fontes,* n. 924.

[51] Cf. Coronata, I, n. 162.

[52] Cf. S.C.S. Off., 5 iul. 1853—*Fontes,* n. 924; S.C.S. Off., litt. 16 mart. 1872—*Fontes,* n. 1021; S.C.S. Off. (Ierosolym.), 14 ian. 1885—*Fontes,* n. 1090.

[53] S.C.S. Off., 5 iul. 1853—*Fontes,* n. 924.

[54] Cf. canon 98, §§ 3, 4.

CONCLUSIONS

1. It is probable that confirmation had begun to be administered apart from baptism as early as the fourth or fifth century.

2. It is probable that sponsors were employed in the rite of confirmation from the time when this sacrament was first conferred separately from the administration of baptism.

3. An interpretation of canon 787 is best derived from a study of the controversy among theologians and canonists as to the nature of the obligation to receive confirmation.

4. The opinion that under ordinary circumstances there exists a grave obligation to receive confirmation cannot be urged in practice.

5. There exists a more compelling obligation to receive confirmation when the danger of death is present than when such a danger is not in evidence.

6. The opinion that the duty of parents to attend to the reception of confirmation on the part of their children is a grave obligation cannot be urged in practice.

7. Provisions should be made, in so far as that is possible, that the insane be given the opportunity to receive confirmation.

8. As a general rule the faithful of this country are probably seriously bound to receive confirmation when the opportunity is provided them.

9. In so far as it is readily possible to have the children do so, they should receive confirmation before they make their first Holy Communion.

10. To require a minimum age of twelve or fourteen for the reception of confirmation in order to keep children in attendance at religious instruction is not justifiable even on the basis of expediency.

11. Only a grave reason would justify the administration of

confirmation to someone who had not been present at the first imposition of hands.

12. The right of the bishop to confer confirmation in the exempt places of his diocese is enjoyed with respect to their own territories by abbots and prelates *nullius,* and probably also by vicars and prefects apostolic.

BIBLIOGRAPHY

Sources

Acta Apostolicae Sedis (*AAS*), Romae, 1909-1929; Civitate Vaticana, 1929-

Acta et Decreta Sacrorum Conciliorum Recentiorum, Collectio Lacensis, 7 vols., Friburgi Brisgoviae, 1870-1890.

Anselm of Lucca, *Collectio Canonum una cum Collectione Minore,* ed. F. Thaner Oeniponte, 1906-1915.

Bouscaren, T. Lincoln, *The Canon Law Digest,* 2 vols., Milwaukee: Bruce Publishing Co., Vol. I, 1934; Vol. II, 1943.

Canones Apostolorum et Conciliorum Saec. IV-VII, ed. H. T. Bruns, 2 vols., Berlin, 1839.

Canones et Decreta Sacrosancti Oecumenici Concilii Tridentini, ed. Neopolitana, 1859.

Catechism of the Council of Trent, The, translated by Very Rev. J. Donovan, Reprint, Dublin: James Duffy and Co., Ltd., 1906.

Codex Iuris Canonici, Pii X Pontificis Maximi iussu digestus, Benedicti Papae XV auctoritate promulgatus, Romae: Typis Polyglottis Vaticanis, 1917. Reimpressio, 1918.

Codicis Iuris Canonici Fontes, cura Emi Petri Card. Gasparri editi, 9 vols., Romae (postea Civitate Vaticana): Typis Polyglottis Vaticanis, 1923-1939. (Vols. VII, VIII, IX ed. cura et studio Emi Iustiniani Card. Serédi.)

Collectanea S. Congregationis de Propaganda Fide, 2 vols., Romae: Typographia Polyglotta S. C. de Propaganda Fide, 1907.

Concilii Plenarii Baltimorensis II Acta et Decreta, Baltimorae: Joannes Murphy, 1868.

Corpus Iuris Canonici, editio Lipsiensis II (Richter-Friedberg), 2 vols., Lipsiae, 1879-1881. Editio anastatice repetita, Lipsiae, 1922.

Corpus Scriptorum Ecclesiasticorum Latinorum, 71 vols., editum consilio et impensis Academiae Litterarum Caesariae Vindobonae, 1866-

Denzinger, Henr., Bannwart, Clem., et Umberg, Joan. B., *Enchiridion Symbolorum Definitionum et Declarationum,* 21-23. ed., Friburgi Brisgoviae: Herder, 1937.

Hardouin, Jean, *Acta Conciliorum et Epistolae Decretales ac Constitutiones Summorum Pontificum,* 12 vols., Parisiis, 1714-1715.

Jaffé, Philippus, *Regesta Pontificum Romanorum ab condita Ecclesia ad annum post Christum MCXCVIII,* 2. ed., G. Wattenbach, F. Kaltenbrunner, P. Ewald, S. Löwenfeld, 2 vols., Lipsiae, 1885-1888.

Kirch, C., *Enchiridion Fontium Historiae Ecclesiasticae Antiquae,* 4. ed., Friburgi Brisgoviae: Herder and Co., 1923.

Mansi, Joannes, *Sanctorum Conciliorum Nova et Amplissima Collectio,* 53 vols. in 60, Parisiis, 1901-1927.

Monumenta Germaniae Historica, Epistolarum Tomus I, Pars I, Gregorii Registrum Lib. I-IV, ed. P. Ewald, Berlin, 1887.

Ordo Romanus I—Mabillon, *Museum Italicum,* 2. ed., 2 vols., Parisiis, 1724.

Pontificale Romanum, Mechliniae, 1845.

The Gelasian Sacramentary, Liber Sacramentorum Romanae Ecclesiae, edited by H. A. Wilson, Oxford, 1894.

Reference Works

Aertnys, J., et Damen, C., *Theologia Moralis secundum S. Alfonsum de Ligorio,* 14. ed., Taurini: Marietti, 1944.

Alphonsus Maria de Ligorio, St., *Theologia Moralis,* 4 vols., ed. L. Gaudé, Romae: Typis Polyglottis Vaticanis, 1905-1912.

Augustine, Charles, *A Commentary on the New Code of Canon Law,* 8 vols., Vol. IV, 3. ed., St. Louis: Herder, 1925.

Ayrinhac, H. A., *Administrative Legislation in the New Code of Canon Law,* London, New York, Toronto: Longmans, Green and Co., 1930.

———, *Legislation on the Sacraments in the New Code of Canon Law,* New York: Longmans, Green and Co., 1928.

Barrett, John D., *A Comparative Study of the Third Plenary Council of Baltimore and the Code,* The Catholic University of America Canon Law Studies, n. 83, Washington, D. C.: The Catholic University of America, 1932.

Benedictus XIV, *De Synodo Dioecesana,* 2 vols., Romae, 1806.

Beste, Udalricus, *Introductio in Codicem,* ed. altera, Collegeville, Minn.: St. John's Abbey Press, 1944.

Billot, L., *De Ecclesiae Sacramentis,* 7. ed., 2 vols., Romae: Pontificia Universitas Gregoriana, 1931.

Blat, Albertus, *Commentarium Textus Codicis Iuris Canonici,* 5 vols. in 6, Romae: Ex Typographia Pontificis in Instituto Pii IX, 1919-1927.

Cappello, Felix M., *Tractatus Canonico-Moralis de Sacramentis,* 5 vols., Vol. I, 5. ed., Taurinorum Augustae: Marietti, 1945.

Cicognani, A., *Canon Law,* authorized English version by J. M. O'Hara and F. J. Brennan, 2. ed., Westminster: The Newman Book Shop, 1946.

Coleman, John J., *The Minister of Confirmation,* The Catholic University of America Canon Law Studies, n. 125, Washington, D. C.: The Catholic University of America Press, 1941.

Coronata, Mattheus Conte a, *Institutiones Iuris Canonici,* 2. ed., 5 vols., Taurini: Marietti, 1939-1947; Vol. II, *De Rebus,* 1939; Vol. IV, *De Delictis et Poenis,* 1945.

———, *Institutiones Iuris Canonici, De Sacramentis Tractatus Canonicus,* 3 vols., Taurini: Marietti, 1943-1946.

Catholic Encyclopedia, The, 15 vols., Index and 2 Suppl., New York, 1907-1922.

D'Ales, Adhemar, *Baptême et Confirmation,* Paris: Librarie, Bloud & Gay, 1928.

Davis, Henry, *Moral and Pastoral Theology,* 4 vols., New York, Sheed and Ward, Inc., 1935.

De Augustinis, Aemilius, *De Re Sacramentaria,* 2. ed., 3 vols., Romae, 1889.

Dens, Petrus, *Tractatus de Sacramentis in Genere et de Sacramentis Baptismi et Confirmationis in Specie,* Mechliniae, 1860.

Diederichs, Michael, *The Jurisdiction of Latin Ordinaries over Their Oriental Subjects,* The Catholic University of America Canon Law Studies, n. 229, Washington, D. C.: The Catholic University of America Press, 1946.

Doronzo, Emmanuel, *De Baptismo et Confirmatione,* Milwaukee: Bruce, 1947.

———, *De Sacramentis in Genere,* Milwaukee: Bruce, 1946.

Duchesne, Louis, *Christian Worship: Its Origin and Evolution,* translated by M. L. McClure, New York, 1903.

Duskie, John, *The Canonical Status of Orientals in the United States,* The Catholic University of America Canon Law Studies, n. 48, Washington, D. C.: The Catholic University of America, 1928.

Farrell, Walter, *A Companion to the Summa,* 4 vols., New York: Sheed and Ward, 1938-1942.

Ferreres, J. B., *Compendium Theologiae Moralis ad Normam Codicis Iuris Canonici,* 14. ed., 2 vols., Romae: Eugenius Subirana, 1928.

Genicot, E., *Institutiones Theologiae Moralis,* 2 vols., Lovanii, 1896-1897.

Genicot, E., et Salsmans, I., *Institutiones Theologiae Moralis,* 10. ed., 2 vols., Bruxellis: Dewit, 1922.

Gury, J. P., *Compendium Theologiae Moralis,* editio in Germania quinta, Ratisbonae, 1874.

Hall, A. C. A., *Confirmation,* London, 1912.

Henry, Joseph, *The Mass and Holy Communion: Interritual Law,* The Catholic University of America Canon Law Studies, n. 235, Washington, D. C.: The Catholic University of America Press, 1946.

Hinschius, Paul, *Decretales Pseudo-Isidorianae et Capitula Angilramni,* Lipsiae, 1863.

Hynes, Harry G., *The Privileges of Cardinals,* The Catholic University of America Canon Law Studies, n. 217, Washington, D. C.: The Catholic University of America Press, 1945.

Jone, H., *Moral Theology,* Englished and adapted to the Code and customs of the United States of America by Rev. Urban Adelman, Westminster: Newman Book Shop, 1945.

Kenrick, Francis P., *Baptism; also a Treatise on Confirmation,* Baltimore, 1852.

———, *Theologia Moralis,* 3 vols., Mechliniae, 1861.

Kilker, Adrian, *Extreme Unction,* The Catholic University of America Canon Law Studies, n. 32, Washington, D. C.: The Catholic University of America, 1926.

Konings, Antonius, *Theologia Moralis,* 5. ed., 2 vols., Neo Eboraci, 1882.

Lahousse, Gustave, *Tractatus de Sacramentis in Genere, de Baptismo, de Confirmatione et de Eucharistia,* Brugis, 1900.

Laras, M., *Confirmation in the Modern World,* translated by George Sayer, New York: Sheed and Ward, 1938.

Laymann, P., *Theologia Moralis,* 2 vols., Patavii, 1733.

Lehmkuhl, Augustinus, *Theologia Moralis,* 9. ed., 2 vols., Friburgi Brisgoviae: Herder, 1898.

Lennerz, H., *De Sacramento Confirmationis,* Romae: Pontificia Universitas Gregoriana, 1945.

Marc, Cl., Gestermann, F. X., et Raus, J. B., *Institutiones Morales Alphonsianae,* 18. ed., 2 vols., Lugduni: Vitte, 1927.

Martène, Edmundus, *De Antiquis Ecclesiae Ritibus,* 3 vols., Rotomagi, 1700.

McCloskey, Joseph, *The Subject of Ecclesiastical Law According to Canon 12,* The Catholic University of America Canon Law Studies, n. 165, Washington, D. C.: The Catholic University of America Press, 1943.

Merkelbach, B., *Summa Theologiae Moralis ad Mentem D. Thomae et ad Normam Iuris Novi,* 3. ed., 3 vols., Parisiis: Typis Desclée, De Brouwer et Soc., 1939.

Migne, Jacques Paul, *Patrologiae Cursus Completus, Series Graeca,* 161 vols., Parisiis, 1857-1866.

———, *Patrologiae Cursus Completus, Series Latina,* 221 vols., Parisiis, 1844-1864.

Mourret, Fernand, *A History of the Catholic Church,* translated by Newton Thompson, 6 vols., St. Louis and London: Herder, 1930-1946.

Nabuco, J., *Pontificalis Romani Expositio Iuridico-Practica,* 3 vols., Petropoli: Editôra Vozes Ltda., 1945.

Noldin, H., Schmitt, A., *Summa Theologiae Moralis,* 26. ed., 3 vols., Ratisbonae: Pustet, 1940.

O'Dwyer, Michael, *Confirmation, A Study in the Development of Sacramental Theology,* New York, 1915.

Pesch, Christianus, *Praelectiones Dogmaticae,* 9 vols., Friburgi Brisgoviae, 1894-1899.

Piscetta, A., et Gennaro, A., *Elementa Theologiae Moralis ad Codicem Iuris Canonici Exacta,* Vol. V, Torino: Società Editrice Internazionale, 1927.

Pistoni, Joseph, *De Confirmatione a Ministro Extraordinario Conferenda,* Città de Vaticano: Libreria Editrice Vaticana, 1947.

Poulet, C., *A History of the Catholic Church,* authorized translation and adaption from the fourth French edition by Rev. Sidney Raemers, 2 vols., St. Louis, London: Herder, 1941-1943.

Pourrat, P., *Theology of the Sacraments, a Study in Positive Theology,* authorized translation from the third French edition, 3. ed., London, St. Louis: B. Herder Book Co., 1924.

Pruemmer, D., *Manuale Iuris Canonici,* 4. and 5. ed., Friburgi Brisgoviae: Herder, 1927.

———, *Manuale Theologiae Moralis Secundum Principia S. Thomae Aquinatis,* 2. et 3. ed., 3 vols., Friburgi Brisgoviae: Herder, 1923.

Ramstein, M., *A Manual of Canon Law,* Hoboken: Terminal Printing and Publishing Co., 1947.

Regatillo, E. F., *Ius Sacramentarium,* 2 vols., Santander: Sal Terrae, 1945-1946.

Reichel, Oswald J., *A Complete Manual of Canon Law,* Vol. I, *The Sacraments,* London: John Hodges, 1896.

Reiffenstuel, Anacletus, *Jus Canonicum Universum,* 5 vols. in 7, Parisiis, 1864-1870.

Sabetti, A., et Barrett, T., *Compendium Theologiae Moralis,* 30. ed., New York, Cincinnati: Pustet, 1924.

Sainte-Beuve, Hieronymus de, *Tractatus de Sacramentis Confirmationis et Unctionis Extremae,* Parisiis, 1686.

Schmalzgrueber, Franciscus, *Jus Ecclesiasticum Universum,* 5 vols. in 12, Romae, 1843-1845.

Suarez, Franciscus, *Opera Omnia,* 26 vols., Parisiis, 1856-1861.

Tanquerey, Adolphus, *Synopsis Theologiae Dogmaticae,* 24. ed., 3 vols., Parisiis-Tornaci (Belg.)-Romae: Desclée et Socii, 1938.

Thomas, Aquinas, St., *Summa Theologica,* 6 vols., Taurini (Italia), Marietti, 1937.

Thomassinus, Ludovicus, *Vetus et Nova Ecclesiae Disciplina,* 3 vols., Venetiis, 1730.

Tournely, Honoratus, *Praelectiones Theologiae de Sacramentis Baptismi et Confirmationis,* Parisiis, 1760.

Van Hove, *Commentarium Lovaniense,* Vol. I, Tom. I, *Prolegomena ad Codicem Iuris Canonici,* 2. ed., Mechliniae-Romae, 1945.

Vermeersch, A., *Theologia Moralis Principia, Responsa, Consilia,* 3. ed. auctior et emendatior, 3 vols., Romae: Università Gregoriana, 1945-1947.

Vermeersch, A., et Creusen, I., *Epitome Iuris Canonici,* 3 vols., Vol. II, 5. ed., Mechliniae-Romae: Dessain, 1934.

Villien, A., *The History and Liturgy of the Sacraments,* English Translation by H. W. Edwards, London: Burns, Oates & Washbourne, Ltd., 1932.

Waldron, Joseph, *The Minister of Baptism,* The Catholic University of America Canon Law Studies, n. 170, Washington, D. C.: The Catholic University of America Press, 1942.

Wernz, F. X., et Vidal, P., *Ius Canonicum,* 7 vols. in 8, Romae: Pontificia Universitas Gregoriana, 1923-1938.

Woywod, Stanislaus, *A Practical Commentary on the Code of Canon Law,* revised by Rev. Callistus Smith, 10. ed., 2 vols., New York: Wagner, 1946.

Zerba, C., *Commentarius in Decretum "Spiritus Sancti Munera,"* Città del Vaticano: Libreria Editrice Vaticana, 1947.

Articles

"Administration of the Sacraments to Dying Non-Catholics," *ER,* LXXXIV (1931), 296-297.

"Administering the Sacraments to Schismatic Children," *ER,* LXXIII (1925), 196.

Bastnagel, C., "Parochial Vicars and the Faculty to Confer Confirmation," *The Jurist,* VII (1947), 174-179.

"Can an Unbaptized Person Receive Confirmation Validly," *ER,* XCII (1935), 192-195.

Cappello, F., "Nonnullae Quaestiones de Confirmatione et Prima Communione," *Periodica,* XVI (1927), 120*-136*.

"Confirmation before First Communion," *ER,* XCVIII (1938), 160-164.

Galtier, P., "L'Age de la Confirmation," *NRT,* LX (1933), 673-686.

Hannan, J., "Decree on the Administration of Confirmation to Those in Danger of Death through Illness," *The Jurist,* VII (1947), 211-233.

"Instructio pro Simplici Sacerdote Sacramentum Confirmationis Sedis Apostolicae Delegatione Administrante: Annotazione," *Il Monitore Ecclesiastico,* XLVII (1935), 111-113.

Kinane, J., "The Age for the Reception of Confirmation," *IER,* 5. series, XL (1932), 638-640.

———, "A Plea for Early Confirmation," *IER,* 5. series, XLI (1933), 307-309.

———, "Early Confirmation of Children," *IER,* 5. series, XLI (1933), 416-417.

King, R., "Confirmation without Previous Baptism by Water," *ER,* LXVI (1922), 75-85.

Maroto, P., "De Aetate Confirmandorum," *Apollinaris,* IV (1931), 372-377.

———, "De Aetate Confirmandorum," *Commentarium pro Religiosis,* XIII (1932), 251-254.

Slater, T., "Sacramental Ministration to Non-Catholics," *ER,* LXIV (1921), 255-260.

Souarn, R., "De Presbytero Orientali Confirmationis Ministro," *Jus Pontificium,"* XI (1931), 133-143.

Woywod, S., "The Legislation of the Code on Confirmation," *The Homiletic and Pastoral Review,* XXI (1920-1921), 105-113.

PERIODICALS

Apollinaris, Romae, 1928-

Clergy Review, The, London, 1931-

Commentarium pro Religiosis, Romae, 1920-; from 1935: *Commentarium pro Religiosis et Missionariis.*

Ecclesiastical Review, The (originally *The American Ecclesiastical Review*), Philadelphia, 1889-1943; Washington, 1944-

Ephemerides Theologicae Lovanienses, Brugis, 1924-

Homiletic and Pastoral Review, The, New York, 1900-

Irish Ecclesiastical Record, The, Dublin, 1864-

Jurist, The, Washington, 1941-

Jus Pontificium, Romae, 1921-1940.

Monitore Ecclesiastico, Il, Romae, 1876-

Nouvelle Revue Théologique, Paris, 1869-

Periodica de Re Canonica et Morali utili Praesertim Religiosis et Clericis, Brugis, 1905-

ABBREVIATIONS

AAS—*Acta Apostolicae Sedis*

Coll. Lac.—*Acta et Decreta Sacrorum Conciliorum Recentiorum, Collectio Lacensis*

CSEL—*Corpus Scriptorum Ecclesiasticorum Latinorum*

ER—Ecclesiastical Review

Fontes—*Codicis Iuris Canonici Fontes, cura* . . . Gasparri editi

Hardouin—*Acta Conciliorum et Epistolae Decretales ac Constitutiones Summorum Pontificum*

IER—*Irish Ecclesiastical Record*

Mansi—*Sanctorum Conciliorum Nova et Amplissima Collectio*

MPL—Migne, *Patrologiae Cursus Completus, Series Latina*

NRT—*Nouvelle Revue Théologique*

Periodica—*Periodica de Re Canonica, Morali, etc.*

S.C.C.—Sacra Congregatio Concilii

S. C. de Prop. Fide—Sacra Congregatio de Propaganda Fide

S.C.S. Off.—Suprema Congregatio Sancti Officii

S.R.C.—Sacrorum Rituum Congregatio

BIOGRAPHICAL NOTE

James Clement Bennington was born on August 8, 1914, at Chester, Pennsylvania. He received his elementary education at St. Michael's and St. Robert's Schools of that city. He was graduated from St. Robert's High School, Chester, in 1931. He entered St. Joseph's College, Philadelphia, Pennsylvania, in the same year, and was graduated with the degree of Bachelor of Arts in 1935. During the next four years he was employed in business and as a part time Instructor in Philosophy at St. Joseph's College. He entered St. Charles' Seminary, Overbrook, Pennsylvania, in September, 1939, and was ordained to the priesthood in February, 1945. After seven months of parish work he entered The Catholic University of America at Washington, D. C., in the fall of 1945. There he obtained the degree of Bachelor of Canon Law in June, 1946, and the degree of Licentiate in Canon Law in June, 1947.

INDEX

CANON LAW STUDIES*

1. Freriks, Rev. Celestine A., C.PP.S., J.C.D., Religious Congregations in Their External Relations, 121 pp. 1916.
2. Galliher, Rev. Daniel M., O.P., J.C.D., Canonical Elections, 117 pp., 1917.
3. Borkowski, Rev. Aurelius L., O.F.M., J.C.D., De Confraternibus Ecclesiasticis, 136 pp., 1918.
4. Castillo, Rev. Cayo, J.C.D., Disertacion Historico-Canonica sobre la Potestad del Cabildo en Sede Vacante o Impedida del Vicario Capitular, 99 pp., 1919 (1918).
5. Kubelbeck, Rev. William J., S.T.B., J.C.D., The Sacred Penitentiaria and Its Relation to Faculties of Ordinaries and Priests, 129 pp., 1918.
6. Petrovits, Rev. Joseph, J.C., S.T.D., J.C.D., The New Church Law on Matrimony, X-461 pp., 1919.
7. Hickey, Rev. John J., S.T.B., J.C.D., Irregularities and Simple Impediments in the New Code of Canon Law, 100 pp., 1920.
8. Klekotka, Rev. Peter J., S.T.B., J.C.D., Diocesan Consultors, 179 pp., 1920.
9. Wanenmacher, Rev. Francis, J.C.D., The Evidence in Ecclesiastical Procedure Affecting the Marriage Bond, 1920 (Printed 1935).
10. Golden, Rev. Henry Francis, J.C.D., Parochial Benefices in the New Code, IV-119 pp., 1921 (Printed 1925).
11. Koudelka, Rev. Charles J., J.C.D., Pastors, Their Rights and Duties According to the New Code of Canon Law, 211 pp., 1921.
12. Melo, Rev. Antonius, O.F.M., J.C.D., De Exemptione Regularium, X-188 pp., 1921
13. Schaaf, Rev. Valentine Theodore, O.F.M., S.T.B., J.C.D., The Cloister, X-180 pp., 1921.
14. Burke, Rev. Thomas Joseph, S.T.D., J.C.D., Competence in Ecclesiastical Tribunals, IV-117 pp., 1922.
15. Leech, Rev. George Leo, J.C.D., A Comparative Study of the Constitution "Apostolicae Sedis" and the "Codex Juris Canonici," 179 pp., 1922.
16. Motry, Rev. Hubert Louis, S.T.D., J.C.D., Diocesan Faculties According to the Code of Canon Law, II-167 pp., 1922.
17. Murphy, Rev. George Lawrence, J.C.D., Delinquencies and Penalties in the Administration and the Reception of the Sacraments, IV-121 pp., 1923.

---

*All published numbers are available from the Catholic University of America Press, 620 Michigan Avenue, N.E., Washington 17, D. C., except the following: Nos. 1-114 inclusive, 116, 118-123, 128, 136, 144, 153, 162, 166, 175, 178, 182 and 198. But the following numbers, now reissued, are obtainable from *The Jurist*, The Catholic University of America, Washington 17, D. C., namely: Nos. 5, 7, 11, 17, 18, 19, 26, 28, 30, 31, 34, 42, 44, 51, 52 and 61.

18. O'Reilly, Rev. John Anthony, S.T.B., J.C.D., Ecclesiastical Sepulture in the New Code of Canon Law, II-129 pp., 1923.
19. Michalicka, Rev. Wenceslas Cyrill, O.S.B., J.C.D., Judicial Procedure in Dismissal of Clerical Exempt Religious, 107 pp., 1923.
20. Dargin, Rev. Edward Vincent, S.T.B., J.C.D., Reserved Cases According to the Code of Canon Law, IV-103 pp., 1924.
21. Godfrey, Rev. John A., S.T.B., J.C.D., The Right of Patronage According to the Code of Canon Law, 153 pp., 1924.
22. Hagedorn, Rev. Francis Edward, J.C.D., General Legislation on Indulgences, II-154 pp., 1924.
23. King, Rev. James Ignatius, J.C.D., The Administration of the Sacraments to Dying Non-Catholics, V-141 pp., 1924.
24. Winslow, Rev. Francis Joseph, O.F.M., J.C.D., Vicars and Prefects Apostolic, IV-149 pp., 1924.
25. Correa, Rev. Jose Servelion, S.T.L., J.C.D., La Potestad Legislativa de la Iglesia Catolica, IV-127 pp., 1925.
26. Dugan, Rev. Henry Francis, A.M., J.C.D., The Judiciary Department of the Diocesan Curia, 87 pp., 1925.
27. Keller, Rev. Charles Frederick, S.T.B., J.C.D., Mass Stipends, 167 pp., 1925.
28. Paschang, Rev. John Linus, J.C.D., The Sacramentals According to the Code of Canon Law, 129 pp., 1925.
29. Piontek, Rev. Cyrillus, O.F.M., S.T.B., J.C.D., De Indulto Exclaustrationis necnon Saecularizationis, XIII-289 pp., 1925.
30. Kearney, Rev. Richard Joseph, S.T.B., J.C.D., Sponsors at Baptism According to the Code of Canon Law, IV-127 pp., 1925.
31. Bartlett, Rev. Chester Joseph, A.M., LL.B., J.C.D., The Tenure of Parochial Property in the United States of America, V-108 pp., 1926.
32. Kilker, Rev. Adrian Jerome, J.C.D., Extreme Unction, V-425 pp., 1926.
33. McCormick, Rev. Robert Emmett, J.C.D., Confessors of Religious, VIII-266 pp., 1926.
34. Miller, Rev. Newton Thomas, J.C.D., Founded Masses According to the Code of Canon Law, VII-93 pp., 1926.
35. Roelker, Rev. Edward G., S.T.D., J.C.D., Principles of Privilege According to the Code of Canon Law, XI-166 pp., 1926.
36. Bakalarczyk, Rev. Richardus, M.I.C., J.U.D., De Novitiatu, VIII-208 pp., 1927.
37. Pizzuti, Rev. Lawrence, O.F.M., J.U.L., De Parochis Religiosis, 1927. (Not Printed.)
38. Bliley, Rev. Nicholas Martin, O.S.B., J.C.D., Altars According to the Code of Canon Law, XIX-132 pp., 1927.
39. Brown, Mr. Brendan Francis, A.B., LL.M., J.U.D., The Canonical Juristic Personality with Special Reference to its Status in the United States of America, V-212 pp., 1927.

40. Cavanaugh, Rev. William Thomas, C.P., J.U.D., The Reservation of the Blessed Sacrament, VIII-101 pp., 1927.
41. Doheny, Rev. William J., C.S.C., A.B., J.C.D., Church Property: Modes of Acquisition, X-118 pp., 1927.
42. Feldhaus, Rev. Aloysius H., C.PP.S., J.C.D., Oratories, IV-141 pp., 1927.
43. Kelly, Rev. James Patrick, A.B., J.C.D., The Jurisdiction of the Simple Confessor, X-208 pp., 1927.
44. Neuberger, Rev. Nicholas J., J.C.D., Canon 6 or the Relation of the Codex Iuris Canonici to the Preceding Legislation, V-95 pp., 1927.
45. O'Keefe, Rev. Gerald Michael, J.C.D., Matrimonial Dispensations, Powers of Bishops, Priests, and Confessors, VIII-232 pp., 1927.
46. Quigley, Rev. Joseph A. M., A.B., J.C.D., Condemned Societies, 139 pp., 1927.
47. Zaplotnik, Rev. Johannes Leo, J.C.D., De Vicariis Foraneis, X-142 pp., 1927.
48. Duskie, Rev. John Aloysius, A.B., J.C.D., The Canonical Status of the Orientals in the United States, VIII-196 pp., 1928.
49. Hyland, Rev. Francis Edward, J.C.D., Excommunication, Its Nature, Historical Development and Effects, VIII-181 pp., 1928.
50. Reimann, Rev. Gerald Joseph, O.M.C., J.C.D., The Third Order Secular of Saint Francis, 201 pp., 1928.
51. Schenk, Rev. Francis J., J.C.D., The Matrimonial Impediments of Mixed Religion and Disparity of Cult, XVI-318 pp., 1929.
52. Coady, Rev. John Joseph, S.T.D., J.U.D., A.M., The Appointment of Pastors, VIII-150 pp., 1929.
53. Kay, Rev. Thomas Henry, J.C.D., Competence in Matrimonial Procedure, VIII-164 pp., 1929.
54. Turner, Rev. Sidney Joseph, C.P., J.U.D., The Vow of Poverty, XLIX-217 pp., 1929.
55. Kearney, Rev. Raymond A., A.B., S.T.D., J.C.D., The Principles of Delegation, VII-149 pp., 1929.
56. Conran, Rev. Edward James, A.B., J.C.D., The Interdict, V-163 pp., 1930.
57. O'Neill, Rev. William H., J.C.D., Papal Rescripts of Favor, VII-218 pp., 1930.
58. Bastnagel, Rev. Clement Vincent, J.U.D., The Appointment of Parochial Adjutants and Assistants, XV-257 pp., 1930.
59. Ferry, Rev. William A., A.B., J.C.D., Stole Fees, V-136 pp., 1930.
60. Costello, Rev. John Michael, A.B., J.C.D., Domicile and Quasi-Domicile, VII-201 pp., 1930.
61. Kremer, Rev. Michael Nicholas, A.B., S.T.B., J.C.D., Church Support in the United States, VI-136 pp., 1930.
62. Angulo, Rev. Luis, C.M., J.C.D., Legislation de la Iglesia sobre la intencion en la application de la Santa Misa, VII-104 pp., 1931.

63. FREY, REV. WOLFGANG NORBERT, O.S.B., A.B., J.C.D., The Act of Religious Profession, VIII-174 pp., 1931.
64. ROBERTS, REV. JAMES BRENDAN, A.B., J.C.D., The Banns of Marriage, XIV-140 pp., 1931.
65. RYDER, REV. RAYMOND ALOYSIUS, A.B., J.C.D., Simony, IX-151 pp., 1931.
66. CAMPAGNA, REV. ANGELO, PH.D., J.U.D., Il Vicario Generale del Vescovo, VII-205, pp., 1931.
67. COX, REV. JOSEPH GODFREY, A.B., J.C.D., The Administration of Seminaries, VI-124 pp., 1931.
68. GREGORY, REV. DONALD J., J.U.D., The Pauline Privilege, XV-165 pp., 1931.
69. DONOHUE, REV. JOHN F., J.C.D., The Impediment of Crime, VII-110 pp., 1931.
70. DOOLEY, REV. EUGENE A., O.M.I., J.C.D., Church Law on Sacred Relics, IX-143 pp., 1931.
71. ORTH, REV. CLEMENT RAYMOND, O.M.C., J.C.D., The Approbation of Religious Institutes, 171 pp., 1931.
72. PERNICONE, REV. JOSEPH M., A.B., J.C.D., The Ecclesiastical Prohibition of Books, XII-267 pp., 1932.
73. CLINTON, REV. CONNELL, A.B., J.C.D., The Paschal Precept, IX-108 pp., 1932.
74. DONNELLY, REV. FRANCIS B., A.M., S.T.L., J.C.D., The Diocesan Synod, VIII-125 pp., 1932.
75. TORRENTE, REV. CAMILO, C.M.F., J.C.D., Las Procesiones Sagradas, V-145 pp., 1932.
76. MURPHY, REV. EDWIN J., C.PP.S., J.C.D., Suspension Ex Informata Conscientia, XI-122 pp., 1932.
77. MACKENZIE, REV. ERIC F., A.M., S.T.L., J.C.D., The Delict of Heresy in its Commission, Penalization, Absolution, VII-124 pp., 1932.
78. LYONS, REV. AVITUS E., S.T.B., J.C.D., The Collegiate Tribunal of First Instance, XI-147 pp., 1932.
79. CONNOLLY, REV. THOMAS A., J.C.D., Appeals, XI-195 pp., 1932.
80. SANGMEISTER, REV. JOSEPH V., A.B., J.C.D., Force and Fear as Precluding Matrimonial Consent, V-211 pp., 1932.
81. JAEGER, REV. LEO A., A.B., J.C.D., The Administration of Vacant and Quasi-Vacant Episcopal Sees in the United States, IX-229 pp., 1932.
82. RIMLINGER, REV. HERBERT T., J.C.D., Error Invalidating Matrimonial Consent, VII-79 pp., 1932.
83. BARRETT, REV. JOHN D. M., S.S., J.C.D., A Comparative Study of the Councils of Baltimore and the Code of Canon Law, IX-223 pp., 1932.
84. CARBERRY, REV. JOHN J., PH.D., S.T.D., J.C.D., The Juridical Form of Marriage, X-177 pp., 1934.
85. DOLAN, REV. JOHN L., A.B., J.C.D., The Defensor Vinculi, XII-157 pp., 1934.

86. HANNAN, REV. JEROME D., A.M., S.T.D., LL.B., J.C.D., The Canon Law of Wills, IX-517 pp., 1934.
87. LEMIEUX, REV. DELISE A., A.M., J.C.D., The Sentence in Ecclesiastical Procedure, IX-131 pp., 1934.
88. O'ROURKE, REV. JAMES J., A.B., J.C.D., Parish Registers, VII-109 pp., 1934.
89. TIMLIN, REV. BARTHOLOMEW, O.F.M., A.M., J.C.D., Conditional Matrimonial Consent, X-381 pp., 1934.
90. WAHL, REV. FRANCIS X., A.B., J.C.D., The Matrimonial Impediments of Consanguinity and Affinity, VI-125 pp., 1934.
91. WHITE, REV. ROBERT J., A.B., LL.B., S.T.B., J.C.D., Canonical Ante-Nuptial Promises and the Civil Law, VI-152 pp., 1934.
92. HERRERA, REV. ANTONIO PARRA, O.C.D., J.C.D., Legislacion Ecclesiastica sobra el Ayuno y la Abstinencia, XI-191 pp., 1935.
93. KENNEDY, REV. EDWIN J., J.C.D., The Special Matrimonial Process in Cases of Evident Nullity, X-165 pp., 1935.
94. MANNING, REV. JOHN J., A.B., J.C.D., Presumption of Law in Matrimonial Procedure, XI-111 pp., 1935.
95. MOEDER, REV. JOHN M., J.C.D., The Proper Bishop for Ordination and Dismissorial Letters, VII-135 pp., 1935.
96. O'MARA, REV. WILLIAM A., A.B., J.C.D., Canonical Causes for Matrimonial Dispensations, IX-155 pp., 1935.
97. REILLY, REV. PETER, J.C.D., Residence of Pastors, IX-81 pp., 1935.
98. SMITH, REV. MARINER T., O.P., S.T.Lr., J.C.D., The Penal Law for Religious, VIII-169 pp., 1935.
99. WHALEN, REV. DONALD W., A.M., J.C.D., The Value of Testimonial Evidence in Matrimonial Procedure, XIII-297 pp., 1935.
100. CLEARY, REV. JOSEPH F., J.C.D., Canonical Limitations on the Alienation of Church Property, VIII-141 pp., 1936.
101. GLYNN, REV. JOHN C., J.C.D., The Promoter of Justice, XX-337 pp., 1936.
102. BRENNAN, REV. JAMES H., S.S., M.A., S.T.B., J.C.D., The Simple Convalidation of Marriage, VI-135 pp., 1937.
103. BRUNINI, REV. JOSEPH BERNARD, J.C.D., The Clerical Obligations of Canons 139 and 142, X-121 pp., 1937.
104. CONNOR, REV. MAURICE, A.B., J.C.D., The Administrative Removal of Pastors, VIII-159 pp., 1937.
105. GUILFOYLE, REV. MERLIN JOSEPH, J.C.D., Custom, XI-144 pp., 1937.
106. HUGHES, REV. JAMES AUSTIN, A.B., A.M., J.C.D., Witnesses in Criminal Trials of Clerics, IX-140 pp., 1937.
107. JANSEN, REV. RAYMOND J., A.B., S.T.L., J.C.D., Canonical Provisions for Catechetical Instruction, VII-153 pp., 1937.
108. KEALY, REV. JOHN JAMES, A.B., J.C.D., The Introductory Libellus in Church Court Procedure, XI-121 pp., 1937.
109. MCMANUS, REV. JAMES EDWARD, C.SS.R., J.C.D., The Administration of Temporal Goods in Religious Institutes, XVI-196 pp., 1937.

110. Moriarty, Rev. Eugene James, J.C.D., Oaths in Ecclesiastical Courts, X-115 pp., 1937.
111. Rainer, Reg. Eligius George, C.SS.R., J.C.D., Suspension of Clerics, XVII-249 pp., 1937.
112. Reilly, Rev. Thomas F., C.SS.R., J.C.D., Visitation of Religious, VI-195 pp., 1938.
113. Moriarty, Rev. Francis E., C.SS.R., J.C.D., The Extraordinary Absolution from Censures, XV-334 pp., 1938.
114. Connolly, Rev. Nicholas P., J.C.D., The Canonical Erection of Parishes, X-132 pp., 1938.
115. Donovan, Rev. James Joseph, J.C.D., The Pastor's Obligation in Prenuptial Investigation, XII-322 pp., 1938.
116. Harrigan, Rev. Robert J., M.A., S.T.B., J.C.D., The Radical Sanation of Invalid Marriages, VIII-208 pp., 1938.
117. Boffa, Rev. Conrad Humbert, J.C.D., Canonical Provisions for Catholic Schools, VII-211 pp., 1939.
118. Parsons, Rev. Anscar John, O.M.Cap., J.C.D., Canonical Elections, XII-236 pp., 1939.
119. Reilly, Rev. Edward Michael, A.B., J.C.D., The General Norms of Dispensation, XII-156 pp., 1939.
120. Ryan, Rev. Gerald Aloysius, A.B., J.C.D., Principles of Episcopal Jurisdiction, XII-172 pp., 1939.
121. Burton, Rev. Francis James, C.S.C., A.B., J.C.D., A Commentary on Canon 1125, X-222 pp., 1940.
122. Miaskiewicz, Rev. Francis Sigismund, J.C.D., Supplied Jurisdiction According to Canon 209, XII-340 pp., 1940.
123. Rice, Rev. Patrick William, A.B., J.C.D., Proof of Death in Prenuptial Investigation, VIII-156 pp., 1940.
124. Anglin, Rev. Thomas Francis, M.S., J.C.D., The Eucharistic Fast, VIII-183 pp., 1941.
125. Coleman, Rev. John Jerome, J.C.D., The Minister of Confirmation, VI-153 pp., 1941.
126. Downs, Rev. John Emmanuel, A.B., J.C.D., The Concept of Clerical Immunity, XI-163 pp., 1941.
127. Esswein, Rev. Anthony Albert, J.C.D., Extrajudicial Penal Powers of Ecclesiastical Superiors, X-144 pp., 1941.
128. Farrell, Rev. Benjamin Francis, M.A., S.T.L., J.C.D., The Rights and Duties of the Local Ordinary Regarding Congregations of Women Religious of Pontifical Approval, V-195 pp., 1941.
129. Feeney, Rev. Thomas John, A.B., S.T.L., J.C.D., Restitutio in Integrum, VI-169 pp., 1941.
130. Findlay, Rev. Stephen William, O.S.B., A.B., J.C.D., Canonical Norms Governing the Deposition and Degradation of Clerics, XVII-279 pp., 1941.
131. Goodwine, Rev. John, A.B., S.T.L., J.C.D., The Right of the Church to Acquire Property, VIII-119 pp., 1941.

132. HESTON, REV. EDWARD LOUIS, C.S.C., PH.D., S.T.D., J.C.D., The Alienation of Church Property in the United States, XII-222 pp., 1941.
133. HOGAN, REV. JAMES JOHN, A.B., S.T.L., J.C.D., Judicial Advocates and Procurators, XIII-200 pp., 1941.
134. KEALY, REV. THOMAS M., A.B., LITT.B., J.C.D., Dowry of Women Religious, IX-152 pp., 1941.
135. KEENE, REV. MICHAEL JAMES, O.S.B., J.C.D., Religious Ordinaries and Canon 198, V-164 pp., 1941 (printed 1942).
136. KERIN, REV. CHARLES A., S.S., M.A., S.T.B., J.C.D., The Privation of Christian Burial, XVI-279 pp., 1941.
137. LOUIS, REV. WILLIAM FRANCIS, M.A., J.C.D., Diocesan Archives, X-101 pp., 1941.
138. MCDEVITT, REV. GILBERT JOSEPH, A.B., J.C.D., Legitimacy and Legitimation, X-247 pp., 1941.
139. MCDONOUGH, REV. THOMAS JOSEPH, A.B., J.C.D., Apostolic Administrators, X-217 pp., 1941.
140. MEIER, REV. CARL ANTHONY, A.B., J.C.D., Penal Administrative Procedure Against Negligent Pastors, XI-240 pp., 1941.
141. SCHMIDT, REV. JOHN ROGG, A.B., J.C.D., The Principles of Authentic Interpretation in Canon 17 of the Code of Canon Law, XII-331 pp., 1941.
142. SLAFKOSKY, REV. ANDREW LEONARD, A.B., J.C.D., The Canonical Episcopal Visitation of the Diocese, X-197 pp., 1941.
143. SWOBODA, REV. INNOCENT ROBERT, O.F.M., J.C.D., Ignorance in Relation to the Imputability of Delicts, IX-271 pp., 1941.
144. DUBÉ, REV. ARTHUR JOSEPH, A.B., J.C.D., The General Principles for the Reckoning of Time in Canon Law, VIII-299 pp., 1941.
145. MCBRIDE, REV. JAMES T., A.B., J.C.D., Incardination and Excardination of Seculars, XX-585 pp., 1941.
146. KRÓL, REV. JOHN T., J.C.D., The Defendant in Ecclesiastical Trials, XII-207 pp., 1942.
147. COMYNS, REV. JOSEPH J., C.SS.R., A.B., J.C.D., Papal and Episcopal Administration of Church Property, XIV-155 pp., 1942.
148. BARRY, REV. GARRETT FRANCIS, O.M.I., J.C.D., Violation of the Cloister, XII-260 pp., 1942.
149. BOLDUC, REV. GATIEN, C.S.V., A.B., S.T.L., J.C.D., Les Études dans les Religious Cléricales, VIII-155 pp., 1942.
150. BOYLE, REV. DAVID JOHN, M.A., J.C.D., The Juridic Effects of Moral Certitude on Pre-Nuptial Guarantees, XII-188 pp., 1942.
151. CANAVAN, REV. WALTER JOSEPH, M.A., LITT.D., J.C.D., The Profession of Faith, XII-143 pp., 1942.
152. DESROCHERS, REV. BRUNO, A.B., PH.L., S.T.B., J.C.D., Le Premier Concile Plénier de Québec et le Code de Droit Canonique, XIV-186 pp., 1942.
153. DILLON, REV. ROBERT EDWARD, A.B., J.C.D., Common Law Marriage, X-148 pp., 1942.

154. DODWELL, REV. EDWARD JOHN, PH.D., S.T.B., J.C.D., The Time and Place for the Celebration of Marriage, X-156 pp., 1942.
155. DONNELLAN, REV. THOMAS ANDREW, A.B., J.C.D., The Obligation of the Missa pro Populo, VII-131 pp., 1942.
156. ELTZ, REV. LOUIS ANTHONY, A.B., J.C.D., Cooperation in Crime, XII-208 pp., 1942.
157. GASS, REV. SYLVESTER FRANCIS, M.A., J.C.D., Ecclesiastical Pensions, XI-206 pp., 1942.
158. GUINIVEN, REV. JOHN JOSEPH, C.SS.R., J.C.D., The Precept of Hearing Mass, XIV-188 pp., 1942.
159. GULCZYNSKI, REV. JOHN THEOPHILUS, J.C.D., The Desecration and Violation of Churches, X-126 pp., 1942.
160. HAMMILL, REV. JOHN LEO, M.A., J.C.D., The Obligations of the Traveler According to Canon 14, VIII-204 pp., 1942.
161. HAYDT, REV. JOHN JOSEPH, A.B., J.C.D., Reserved Benefices, XI-148 pp., 1942.
162. HUSER, REV. ROGER JOHN, O.F.M., A.B., J.C.D., The Crime of Abortion in Canon Law, XII-187 pp., 1942.
163. KEARNEY, REV. FRANCIS PATRICK, A.B., S.T.L., J.C.D., The Principles of Canon Law 1127, X-162 pp., 1942.
164. LINAHEN, REV. LEO JAMES, S.T.L., J.C.D., De Absolutione Complicis in Peccato Turpi, V-114 pp., 1942.
165. MCCLOSKEY, REV. JOSEPH ALOYSIUS, A.B., J.C.D., The Subject of Ecclesiastical Law According to Canon 12, XVII-246 pp., 1942 (printed 1943).
166. O'NEILL, REV. FRANCIS JOSEPH, C.SS.R., J.C.D., The Dismissal of Religious in Temporary Vows, XIII-220 pp., 1942.
167. PRINCE, REV. JOHN EDWARD, A.B., S.T.B., J.C.D., The Diocesan Chancellor, X-136 pp., 1942.
168. RIESNER, REV. ALBERT JOSEPH, C.SS.R., J.C.D., Apostates and Fugitives from Religious Institutes, IX-168 pp., 1942.
169. STENGER, REV. JOSEPH BERNARD, J.C.D., The Mortgaging of Church Property, 186 pp., 1942.
170. WALDRON, REV. JOSEPH FRANCIS, A.B., J.C.D., The Minister of Baptism, XII-197 pp., 1942.
171. WILLETT, REV. ROBERT ALBERT, J.C.D., The Probative Value of Documents in Ecclesiastical Trials, X-124 pp., 1942.
172. WOEBER, REV. EDWARD MARTIN, M.A., J.C.D., The Interpellations, XII-161 pp., 1942.
173. BENKO, REV. MATTHEW ALOYSIUS, O.S.B., M.A., J.C.D., The Abbot *Nullius,* XVI-148 pp., 1943.
174. CHRIST, REV. JOSEPH JAMES, M.A., S.T.L., J.C.D., Dispensation from Vindicative Penalties, XIV-285 pp., 1943.
175. CLANCY, REV. PATRICK M. J., O.P., A.B., S.T.Lr., J.C.D., The Local Religious Superior, X-229 pp., 1943.
176. CLARKE, REV. THOMAS JAMES, J.C.D., Parish Societies, XII-147 pp., 1943.

177. Connolly, Rev. John Patrick, S.T.L., J.C.D., Synodical Examiners and Parish Priest Consultors, X-223 pp., 1943.
178. Drumm, Rev. William Martin, A.B., J.C.D., Hospital Chaplains, XII-175 pp., 1943.
179. Flanagan, Rev. Bernard Joseph, A.B., S.T.L., J.C.D., The Canonical Erection of Religious Houses, X-147 pp., 1943.
180. Kelleher, Rev. Stephen Joseph, A.B., S.T.B., J.C.D., Discussions with Non-Catholics: Canonical Legislation, X-93 pp., 1943.
181. Lewis, Rev. Gordian, C.P., J.C.D., Chapters in Religious Institutes, XII-169 pp., 1943.
182. Marx, Rev. Adolph, J.C.D., The Declaration of Nullity of Marriages Contracted Outside the Church, X-151 pp., 1943.
183. Matulenas, Rev. Raymond Anthony, O.S.B., A.B., J.C.D., Communication, a Source of Privileges, VII-225 pp., 1943.
184. O'Leary, Rev. Charles Gerard, C.SS.R., J.C.D., Religious Dismissed After Perpetual Profession, X-213 pp., 1943.
185. Power, Rev. Cornelius Michael, J.C.D., The Blessing of Cemeteries, XII-231 pp., 1943.
186. Shuhler, Rev. Ralph Vincent, O.S.A., J.C.D., Privileges of Religious to Absolve and Dispense, XII-195 pp., 1943.
187. Ziolkowski, Rev. Thaddeus Stanislaus, A.B., J.C.D., The Consecration and Blessing of Churches, XII-151 pp., 1943.
188. Heneghan, Rev. John Joseph, S.T.D., J.C.D., The Marriages of Unworthy Catholics: Canons 1065 and 1066, XVI-213 pp., 1944.
189. Carroll, Rev. Coleman Francis, M.A., S.T.L., J.C.L., Charitable Institutions.
190. Ciesluk, Rev. Joseph Edward, Ph.B., S.T.L., J.C.D., National Parishes in the United States, VI-178 pp., 1944.
191. Coburn, Rev. Vincent Paul, A.B., J.C.D., Marriages of Conscience, XII-172 pp., 1944.
192. Connors, Rev. Charles Paul, C.S.Sp., A.B., J.C.D., Extra-Judicial Procurators in the Code of Canon Law, X-94 pp., 1944.
193. Coyle, Rev. Paul Raymond, A.B., J.C.D., Judicial Exceptions, X-142 pp., 1944.
194. Fair, Rev. Bartholomew Francis, A.B., S.T.L., J.C.D., The Impediment of Abduction, XII-122 pp., 1944.
195. Gallagher, Rev. Thomas Raphael, O.P., A.B., S.T.Lr., J.C.D., The Examination of the Qualities of the Ordinand, X-166 pp., 1944.
196. Gannon, Rev. John Mark, S.T.L., J.C.D., The Interstices Required for the Promotion to Orders, XII-100 pp., 1944.
197. Goldsmith, Rev. J. William, B.C.S., S.T.L., J.C.D., The Competence of Church and State Over Marriages—Disputed Points, X-128 pp., 1944.
198. Goodwine, Rev. Joseph Gerard, A.B., S.T.B., J.C.D., The Reception of Converts, XIV-326 pp., 1944.

199. KOWALSKI, REV. ROMUALD EUGENE, O.F.M., A.B., J.C.D., Sustenance of Religious Houses of Regulars, X-174 pp., 1944.
200. MCCOY, REV. ALAN EDWARD, O.F.M., J.C.D., Force and Fear in Relation to Delictual Imputability and Penal Responsibility, XII-160 pp., 1944.
201. MCDEVITT, REV. VINCENT JOHN, PH.B., S.T.L., J.C.L., Perjury.
202. MARTIN, REV. THOMAS OWEN, PH.D., S.T.D., J.C.D., Adverse Possession, Prescription and Limitation of Actions: The Canonical "Praescriptio," XX-208 pp., 1944.
203. MIKLOSOVIC, REV. PAUL JOHN, A.B., J.C.L., Attempted Marriages and Their Consequent Juridic Effects.
204. MUNDY, REV. THOMAS MAURICE, A.B., S.T.L., J.C.D., The Union of Parishes, X-164 pp. 1944.
205. O'DEA, REV. JOHN COYLE, A.B., J.C.D., The Matrimonial Impediment of Nonage, VIII-126 pp., 1944.
206. OLALIA, REV. ALEXANDER AYSON, S.T.L., J.C.D., A Comparative Study of the Christian Constitution of States and the Constitution of the Philippine Commonwealth, XII-136 pp., 1944.
207. POISSON, REV. PIERRE-MARIE, C.S.C., A.B., PH.L., TH.L., J.C.L., Droits Patrimoniaux des Maisons et des Eglises Religieuses.
208. STADALNIKAS, REV. CASIMIR JOSEPH, M.I.C., J.C.D., Reservation of Censures, X-141 pp., 1944.
209. SULLIVAN, REV. EUGENE HENRY, S.T.L., J.C.D., Proof of the Reception of the Sacraments, X-165 pp., 1944.
210. VAUGHAN, REV. WILLIAM EDWARD, J.C.D., Constitutions for Diocesan Courts, X-200 pp., 1944.
211. PARO, REV. GINO, S.T.D., J.C.D., The Right of Papal Legation, X-221 pp., 1944 (printed 1947).
212. BALZER, REV. RALPH FRANCIS, C.P., J.C.D., The Computation of Time in a Canonical Novitiate, X-227 pp., 1945.
213. DOUGHERTY, REV. JOHN WHELAN, A.B., S.T.L., J.C.D., De Inquisitione Speciali, XII-195 pp., 1945.
214. DZIOB, REV. MICHAEL WALTER, J.C.D., The Sacred Congregation for the Oriental Church, XII-181 pp., 1945.
215. EIDENSCHINK, REV. JOHN ALBERT, O.S.B., B.A., J.C.D., The Election of Bishops in the Letters of Pope Gregory the Great, VIII-200 pp., 1945.
216. GILL, REV. NICHOLAS, C.P., J.C.D., The Spiritual Prefect in Clerical Religious Houses of Study, X-140 pp., 1945.
217. HYNES, REV. HARRY GERARD, S.T.L., J.C.D., The Privileges of Cardinals, XII-183 pp., 1945.
218. MCDEVITT, REV. GERALD VINCENT, S.T.L., J.C.D., The Renunciation of an Ecclesiastical Office, XIV-179 pp., 1945.
219. MANNING, REV. JOSEPH LEROY, J.C.D., The Free Conferral of Offices, VII-116 pp., 1945.

220. Meyer, Rev. Louis G., O.S.B., A.B., S.T.B., J.C.D., Alms-gathering by Religious, XII-163 pp., 1945.
221. O'Donnell, Rev. Cletus Francis, M.A., J.C.D., The Marriage of Minors, XII-268 pp., 1945.
222. Prunskis, Rev. Joseph, J.C.D., Comparative Law, Ecclesiastical and Civil, in Lithuanian Concordat, X-161 pp., 1945.
223. Sweeney, Rev. Francis Patrick, C.SS.R., J.C.D., The Reduction of Clerics to the Lay State, X-199 pp., 1945.
224. Vogelpohl, Rev. Henry John, J.C.D., The Simple Impediments to Holy Orders, XVI-190 pp., 1945.
225. Brockhaus, Rev. Thomas Aquinas, O.S.B., J.C.D., Religious who are known as *Conversi*, X-127 pp., 1945.
226. Griese, Rev. Orville Nicholas, S.T.D., J.C.D., The Marriage Contract and the Procreation of Offspring, XVI-224 pp., 1946.
227. Boudreaux, Rev. Warren Louis, J.C.D., The *"ab acatholicis nati"* of Canon 1099, § 2, XII-110 pp., 1946.
228. Bowe, Rev. Thomas Joseph, A.B., J.C.D., Religious Superioresses, VIII-206 pp., 1946.
229. Diederichs, Rev. Michael Ferdinand, S.C.J., J.C.D., The Jurisdiction of the Latin Ordinaries over their Oriental Subjects, XIV-153 pp., 1946.
230. Dingman, Rev. Maurice John, A.B., S.T.L., J.C.L., The Plaintiff in Contentious Trials.
231. Frison, Rev. Basil, C.M.F., M.Mus., J.C.D., The Retroactivity of Law, X-221 pp., 1946.
232. Galvin, Rev. William Anthony, M.A., J.C.D., The Administrative Transfer of Pastors, XII-288 pp., 1946.
233. Goracy, Rev. Joseph C., J.C.L., The Diriment Matrimonial Impediment of Major Orders.
234. Hale, Rev. Joseph Francis, M.A., S.T.L., J.C.D., The Pastor of Burial, X-247 pp., 1946 (printed 1949).
235. Henry, Rev. Joseph Arthur, A.B., J.C.D., The Mass and Holy Communion: Interritual Law, XII-138 pp., 1946.
236. Linenberger, Rev. Herbert, C.PP.S., J.C.D., The False Denunciation of an Innocent Confessor, VIII-205 pp., 1946 (1949).
237. Lowry, Rev. James Martin, A.B., J.C.D., Dispensation from Private Vows, XII-266 pp., 1946.
238. Lynch, Rev. George Edward, A.B., S.T.L., J.C.D., Coadjutors and Auxiliaries of Bishops, X-107 pp., 1946 (printed 1947).
239. Lynch, Rev. Timothy, M.S.SS.T., J.C.D., Contracts between Bishops and Religious Congregations, XIII-232 pp., 1946.
240. McClunn, Rev. Justin David, A.B., S.T.L., J.C.D., Administrative Recourse, VII-142 pp., 1946.
241. Lohmuller, Rev. Martin Nicholas, A.B., J.C.D., The Promulgation of Law, XII-140 pp., 1947.

242. McGrath, Rev. James, A.B., J.C.D., The Privilege of the Canon, XII-156 pp., 1946.
243. Marbach, Rev. Joseph Francis, A.B., J.C.D., Marriage Legislation for the Catholics of the Oriental Rites in the United States and Canada, XIV-314 pp., 1946.
244. Shimkus, Rev. Bernard Aloysius, A.B., J.C.L., The Determination and Transfer of Rite.
245. Smith, Rev. Vincent Michael, A.B., S.T.L., J.C.D., Ignorance Affecting Matrimonial Consent, X-118 pp., 1946 (printed 1950).
246. Wachtrle, Rev. Paul Anthony, A.B., J.C.L., The Baptism of the Children of Non-Catholics.
247. Crotty, Rev. Matthew Michael, J.C.D., The Recipient of First Holy Communion, X-142 pp., 1947.
248. Eagleton, Rev. George, J.C.D., The Quinquennial Faculties, Formula IV, XIV-199 pp., 1947 (printed 1948).
249. Gibbons, Rev. Marion Leo, C.M., J.C.L., Domicile of the Wife Unlawfully Separated from Her Husband, XIV-171 pp., 1947.
250. Kelly, Rev. Bernard M., S.T.L., J.C.D., The Functions Reserved to Pastors, XII-141 pp., 1947.
251. Kilcullen, Rev. Thomas J., LL.M., J.C.D., The Collegiate Moral Person as Party Litigant, X-150 pp., 1947.
252. Lafontaine, Rev. Germaine Joseph, W.F., J.C.D., Relations Canoniques entre le Missionaire et Ses Superieurs, X-117 pp., 1947.
253. Lane, Rev. Loras Thomas, A.B., S.T.L., J.C.D., Matrimonial Procedure in the Ordinary Court of Second Instance, XVI-184 pp., 1947.
254. Lover, Rev. James Francis, C.Ss.R., J.C.D., The Master of Novices, X-168 pp., 1947.
255. McNicholas, Rev. Timothy Joseph, J.C.D., The *Septimae Manus* Witness, XII-133 pp., 1947 (printed 1949).
256. Marositz, Rev. Joseph John, M.S.C., J.C.D., Obligations and Privileges of Religious Promoted to the Episcopal or Cardinalitial Dignities, XII-180 pp., 1947.
257. Murphy, Rev. Francis Joseph, J.C.D., Legislative Powers of the Provincial Council, XII-158 pp., 1947.
258. O'Brien, Rev. Romaeus William, O.Carm., J.C.D., The Provincial Superior in Religious Orders of Men, X-294 pp., 1947.
259. Pfaller, Rev. Benedict Anthony, O.S.B., J.C.D., *The ipso facto* Effected Dismissal of Religious, XII-225 pp., 1947.
260. Popek, Rev. Alphonse Sylvester, J.C.D., The Rights and Obligations of Metropolitans, XX-460 pp., 1947.
261. Ristuccia, Rev. Bernard Joseph, C.M., J.C.D., Quasi-Religious, XVI-318 pp., 1947 (printed 1949).
262. Sonntag, Rev. Nathaniel Louis, O.F.M.Cap., J.C.D., Censorship of Special Classes of Books, XII-147 pp., 1947.
263. Stadler, Rev. Joseph Nicholas, J.C.D., Frequent Holy Communion, X-158 pp., 1947.

264. Szal, Rev. Ignatius Joseph, J.C.D., The Communication of Catholics with Schismatics, XII-217 pp., 1947.
265. Wagner, Rev. Urban S., O.F.M., Conv., J.C.D., Parochial Substitute Vicars and Supplying Priests, IX-126 pp., 1947.
266. Quinn, Rev. Joseph, M.A., J.C.D., Documents Required for the Reception of Orders, XIV-207 pp., 1948.
267. Bennington, Rev. James Clement, A.B., J.C.L., The Recipient of Confirmation.
268. Blaher, Rev. Damian Joseph, O.F.M., A.B., J.C.D., The Ordinary Processes in Causes of Beatification and Canonization, XVI-290 pp., 1948 (printed 1949).
269. Clune, Rev. Robert Bell, B.A., J.C.D., The Judicial Interrogation of the Parties, XII-142 pp., 1948.
270. Courtemanche, Rev. Basil F., B.A., J.C.D., The Total Simulation of Matrimonial Consent, XX-120 pp., 1948.
271. Dlouhy, Rev. Maur John, O.S.B., A.B., J.C.L., The Ordination of Exempt Religious.
272. Donovan, Rev. John Thomas, Ph.B., S.T.L., J.C.D., The Clerical Obligation of Canons 138 and 140, XII-209 pp., 1948.
273. Freking, Rev. Frederick W., A.B., S.T.B., J.C.D., The Canonical Installation of Pastors, XII-210 pp., 1948.
274. Fulton, Rev. Thomas B., J.C.D., Prenuptial Investigation, XII-190 pp., 1948.
275. Godley, Rev. James P., J.C.D., Time and Place for the Celebration of Mass, X-206 pp., 1948 (printed 1949).
276. Kane, Rev. Thomas A., A.B., B.S., J.C.D., Jurisdiction of the Patriarchs of the Major Sees in Antiquity and in the Middle Ages, XII-111 pp., 1948 (printed 1949).
277. Kennedy, Rev. Andrew A., J.C.L., The Annual Pastoral Report to the Local Ordinary.
278. Konrad, Rev. Joseph George, J.C.D., Transfer of Religious to Another Community, VIII-284 pp., 1948 (printed 1949).
279. Kress, Rev. Alphonse, J.C.L., Contumacy in Ecclesiastical Trials.
280. McCartney, Rev. Marcellus Anthony, O.F.M., M.A., J.C.D., Faculties of Regular Confessors, XII-164 pp., 1948 (printed 1949).
281. McCaslin, Rev. Edward Patrick, M.A., S.T.L., J.C.L., The Division of Parishes.
282. McElroy, Rev. Francis J., A.B., J.C.D., The Privileges of Bishops, XII-142 pp., 1948 (printed 1951).
283. Quinn, Rev. Stephen, M.S.SS.T., J.C.D., Relation Between the Local Ordinary and Religious of Diocesan Approval, XII-153 pp., 1948 (printed 1949).
284. Schneider, Rev. Edelhard Louis, S.D.S., B.A., J.C.L., The Status of Secularized Ex-Religious Clerics, X-155 pp., 1948.
285. Thompson, Chester J., A.B., J.C.D., The Simple Removal from Office, XII-141 pp., 1948 (printed 1951).

www.ingramcontent.com/pod-product-compliance
Lightning Source LLC
LaVergne TN
LVHW050223080826
844660LV00012B/459